3rd Edition

Travel better, enjoy more

Authors	**Computer Graphics**	**Artistic Director**
Pierre Longnus	Stéphanie Routhier	Patrick Farei (Atoll)
Paul-Éric Dumontier		
François Rémillard	**Translation**	**Illustrations**
Collaboration	Jennifer McMorran	Lorette Pierson
Clayton Anderson	Tracy Kendrick	Myriam Gagné
	Danielle Gauthier	
Editor	Emmy Pahmer	**Photography**
Stéphane G.		*Cover Page*
Marceau	**Page Layout**	Jürgen Vogt/
	Typesetting	The Image Bank
Publisher	Isabelle Lalonde	*Inside Pages*
Pascale Couture	*Visuals*	Reflexion:
	Anne Joyce	Troy & Mary Parlee
Copy Editing	Julie Brodeur	Tibor Bognàr
Wayne Hiltz		Sean O'Neill
Anne Joyce	**Cartographers**	Sheila Naiman
Editing Assistance	Isabelle Lalonde	Walter Bibikow
Dena Duijkers	Patrick Thivierge	Megapress Images:
Kate Walker	Yanik Landreville	P. Brunet
	Brad Fenton	C. Moreno

OFFICES
CANADA: Ulysses Travel Guides, 4176 Rue St-Denis, Montréal, Québec, H2W 2M5,
☎ (514) 843-9447 or 1-877-542-7247, ⊜(514) 843-9448, info@ulysses.ca,
www.ulyssesguides.com

EUROPE: Les Guides de Voyage Ulysse SARL, BP 159, 75523 Paris Cedex 11, France,
☎ 01 43 38 89 50, ⊜01 43 38 89 52, voyage@ulysse.ca, www.ulyssesguides.com

U.S.A.: Ulysses Travel Guides, 305 Madison Avenue, Suite 1166, New York, NY 10165,
☎ 1-877-542-7247, info@ulysses.ca, www.ulyssesguides.com

DISTRIBUTORS
CANADA: Ulysses Books & Maps, 4176 Saint-Denis, Montréal, Québec, H2W 2M5,
☎ (514) 843-9882, ext.2232, 800-748-9171, Fax: 514-843-9448, info@ulysses.ca,
www.ulyssesguides.com

GREAT BRITAIN AND IRELAND: World Leisure Marketing, Unit 11, Newmarket Court,
Newmarket Drive, Derby DE24 8NW, ☎ 1 332 57 37 37, Fax: 1 332 57 33 99
office@wlmsales.co.uk

SCANDINAVIA: Scanvik, Esplanaden 8B, 1263 Copenhagen K, DK, ☎ (45) 33.12.77.66,
Fax: (45) 33.91.28.82

SPAIN: Altaïr, Balmes 69, E-08007 Barcelona, ☎ 454 29 66, Fax: 451 25 59,
altair@globalcom.es

SWITZERLAND: OLF, P.O. Box 1061, CH-1701 Fribourg, ☎ (026) 467.51.11,
Fax: (026) 467.54.66

U.S.A.: The Globe Pequot Press, 246 Goose Lane, Guilford, CT 06437 - 0480,
☎1-800-243-0495, Fax: 800-820-2329, sales@globe-pequot.com

Other countries, contact Ulysses Books & Maps, 4176 Rue Saint-Denis, Montréal, Québec,
H2W 2M5, ☎ (514) 843-9882, ext.2232, 800-748-9171, Fax: 514-843-9448, info@ulysses.ca,
www.ulyssesguides.com

Canadian Cataloguing in Publication Data (see page 8)
© July 2000, Ulysses Travel Guides.
All rights reserved Printed in Canada, ISBN 2-89464-243-1

*"It has the combined excellence of Nature's gift
and man's handiwork."*

Stephen Leacock on Vancouver
in *My Discovery of the West* (1937)

Table of Contents

List of Maps

Map Symbols

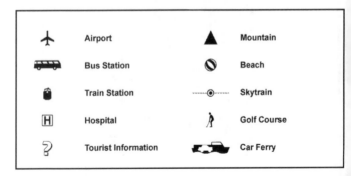

✈	Airport	▲	Mountain
🚌	Bus Station	Ø	Beach
🚆	Train Station	·····◉·····	Skytrain
H	Hospital	🏌	Golf Course
?	Tourist Information	🚢	Car Ferry

Symbols

Symbol	Meaning
(ship)	Ulysses's Favourite
☎	Telephone Number
	Fax Number
&	Wheelchair Accessible
✕	Pets Allowed
P	Parking
≡	Air Conditioning
⊗	Fan
≈	Pool
ℜ	Restaurant
⊙	Whirlpool
ℝ	Refrigerator
K	Kitchenette
△	Sauna
⊘	Exercise Room
tv	Colour Television
pb	Private Bathroom
sb	Shared Bathroom
bkfst incl.	Breakfast Included

ATTRACTION CLASSIFICATION

★	Interesting
★★	Worth a visit
★★★	Not to be missed

The prices listed in this guide are for the admission of one adult.

HOTEL CLASSIFICATION

The prices in the guide are for one room,
double occupancy in high season.

RESTAURANT CLASSIFICATION

$	$10 or less
$$	$10 to $20
$$$	$20 to $30
$$$$	$30 and more

The prices in the guide are for a meal for one
person, not including drinks and tip.

All prices in this guide are in Canadian dollars.

Write to Us

Cataloguing

Canadian Cataloguing in Publication Data

Main entry under title

Vancouver

(Ulysses travel guide)

ISSN 1486-360X
ISBN 2-89464-243-1

1. Vancouver (B.C.) - Guidebooks. I. Title. II. Series

FC3847.18.D8513 2000 917.11'33044   C99-301652-9

Thanks

We acknowledge the financial support of the Government of Canada through the Book Publishing Industry Development Program (BPIDP) for our publishing activities.

We would also like to thank SODEC (Québec) for its financial support.

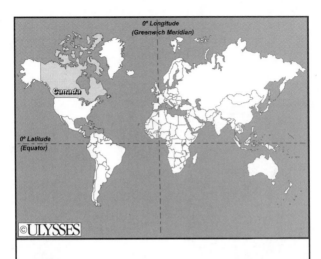

Where is Vancouver?

British Columbia
Capital: Victoria
Population: 3,900,000 inhab.
Area: 950,000km²
Currency: Canadian Dollar

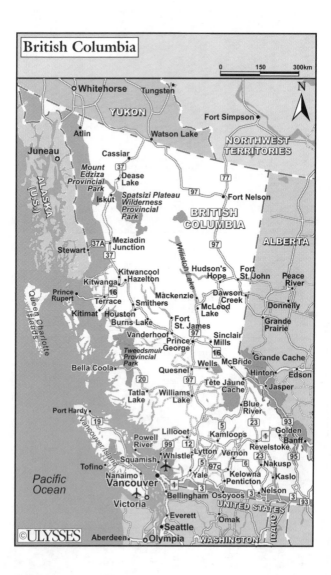

British Columbia

0   150   300km

N

Whitehorse   Tungsten

YUKON

Atlin   Fort Simpson

Watson Lake

NORTHWEST
TERRITORIES

Cassiar

Juneau

Mount
Edziza   Dease
Provincial   Lake
Park   Spatsizi Plateau   97
Iskut   Wilderness   Fort Nelson
                Provincial
                Park   BRITISH
                                  COLUMBIA

ALASKA
(U.S.)

37A   Meziadin
      Junction   ALBERTA
Stewart
      37   97
                   Kitwancool   Hudson's   Fort
                   Hazelton   Hope   St. John   Peace
      Kitwanga   River
Prince   16   Mackenzie   Dawson
Rupert   Terrace   McLeod   Creek
      Kitimat   Houston   Fort Lake   Donnelly
               Burns Lake   St. James   Grande
          Vanderhoof   97   Sinclair   Prairie
                   Prince   Mills
Queen Charlotte Islands George 16   Grande Cache
          Tweedsmuir   McBride
          Provincial   Wells
Bella Coola Park   Quesnel   Hinton
                                97   Tête Jaune   Edson
          Tatla   Williams   Cache   Jasper
          Lake   Lake   Blue
                   20   River
Port Hardy 19   23   93
                       Lillooet Kamloops Golden
          Powell   5   23   1   Banff
Vancouver Island River 99 12   Revelstoke 95
          Squamish Whistler Lytton Vernon   Nakusp
Tofino   5   97c Yale Kelowna Kaslo
Pacific   Nanaimo   Penticton
Ocean   Vancouver   1   3   Nelson
               Bellingham Osoyoos 3   3
          Victoria   UNITED STATES   93
                   Everett
                   Seattle   Omak   IDAHO
©ULYSSES Aberdeen Olympia WASHINGTON

Willston Lake

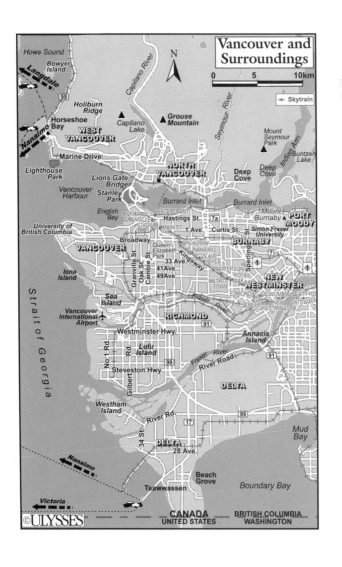

Vancouver and Surroundings

0   5   10km

⟶ Skytrain

Howe Sound
Bowyer Island
Langdale
99
Holiburn Ridge
Horseshoe Bay
WEST VANCOUVER
Capilano Lake
Grouse Mountain
Capilano River
Seymour River
Mount Seymour Park
Buntzen Lake
Indian Arm
Nanaimo
Marine Drive
Lighthouse Park
Lions Gate Bridge
Vancouver Harbour
Stanley Park
NORTH VANCOUVER
Deep Cove
Deep Cove
English Bay
Burrard Inlet
Burrard Inlet
University of British Columbia
BURRARD
WATERFRONT
GRANVILLE
STADIUM
Hastings St.
7a
Mount Burnaby
PORT MOODY
MAIN ST.
1 Ave.
Curtis St.
Simon Fraser University
Broadway
BROADWAY
VANCOUVER
Queen Elizabeth Park
NANAIMO
29 AVE.
JOYCE
BURNABY
PATTERSON
Sperling
1
Granville St.
Oak St.
Cambie St.
33 Ave.
41Ave.
49Ave.
Kingsway
ROYAL
METRO TOWN
EDMONDS
COLUMBIA
SCOTT RD.
NEW WESTMINSTER
1
Iona Island
Sea Island
Vancouver International Airport
METRO TOWN
STREET
NEW WESTMINSTER GATEWA
Westminster Hwy.
RICHMOND
91
Annacis Island
No. 1 Rd.
Gilbert Rd.
Lulu Island
Fraser River
River Road
91
Steveston Hwy.
99
DELTA
Strait of Georgia
Westham Island
River Rd.
17
99
Mud Bay
34 St.
DELTA
28 Ave.
Beach Grove
Boundary Bay
Nanaimo
Victoria
Tsawwassen
©ULYSSES
CANADA
UNITED STATES
BRITISH COLUMBIA
WASHINGTON

Portrait

Vancouver is truly a new city, one framed by the mighty elements of sea and mountains.

As part of one of the most isolated reaches on the planet for many years, over the last 100 years the city has developed close ties with the nations of the largest ocean on Earth, and is fast becoming the multicultural metropolis of the Pacific Rim.

Although its history is tied to the development of British Columbia's natural resources, most residents were lured here by the magnificent setting and the climate which is remarkably mild in a country known for its bitter winters and stifling summers. Vancouver, where Asia meets America, is a city well worth discovering.

Geography

Canada's West coast, bounded by the 49th paral-lel to the south and the Alaskan border to the north, is dominated by the Coast Mountains, a chain of peaks west of the Rockies that form an almost unbroken barrier between the Pacific and the hinterland. The vast delta of the Fraser River does break it and thus proves suitable for human habitation; Vancouver was founded in this favourable location. The city is now the third largest in Canada with a population of nearly two million in the metropolitan area. It is also the only major city in the country whose eyes are decidedly turned toward the Pacific.

Pacific-minded though it is, Vancouver does not actually face right onto the ocean, but is separated from the sea by Vancouver Island where Victoria, the capital of British Columbia, is located. Vancouver, the province's economic hub, lies on the Strait of Georgia, an arm of the sea separating Vancouver Island from the mainland. Its population is scattered across two peninsulas formed by Burrard Inlet to the north and False Creek to the south.

Point Grey, the larger and more southerly end, is home to the University of British Columbia and sprawling residential neighbourhoods. On the smaller point to the north, visitors will discover a striking contrast between the east end with its cluster of downtown skyscrapers, and the west end that's occupied by the lovely, unspoiled woodlands of Stanley Park. The city's location, surrounded by water and connected to the rest of the country by bridges and ferries, has led to a steady increase in the price of land in the centre and to major traffic prob-

lems for commuters from the city's suburbs and satellite towns. Finally, it is worth noting that Vancouver is only about 30km from the U.S. border (and less than 200km north of Seattle).

Vancouver boasts an exceptionally mild climate with average temperatures of 3°C in January and 17°C in July. There is very little snow, though there is a lot of rain (annual average: 163 days of precipitation) and the summers are temperate and sunny. Clouds that form over the ocean are blown inland by westerly winds. When they hit the Coast Mountains, they precipitate and cause generally grey weather.

Plants thrive in this wet climate. Its wide variety of trees and flowers make Vancouver a vast, luxuriant garden where everything grows to be that much bigger than elsewhere. Not only are there species indigenous to the temperate rain forest (the northern counterpart of the tropical forest) like enormous Douglas firs, red cedars, giant thuyas, and western hemlocks, but over the decades countless European and Asian plants have been imported to satisfy the local residents' passion for gardening. The numerous private and public ornamental gardens in and around Vancouver are thus adorned with North American, European and Asian species, to name but a few.

History and Economic Development

Aboriginal Peoples

Over 10,000 years ago, a number of tribes travelled across the Bering Strait from Asia and scattered across North America (their history all but disappeared along with the ice that once covered a large part of the northern hemisphere). They formed the numerous Aboriginal nations and pre-Columbian civilizations of this continent. There is some doubt, however, as to whether or not Aboriginal civilization on the West Coast originated with these vast waves of immigration. According to one theory, the ancestors of the West Coast tribes came here more recently (around 3000 BC) from islands in the Pacific. Proponents of this hypothesis base their argument on the Aboriginal peoples' art, traditions and spoken languages which are not unlike those of the indige-

nous peoples of the Pacific islands. When the first Europeans arrived here in the late 18th century, the region that would become Vancouver was inhabited by the Salish (the other Aboriginal language families on the Pacific coast are Haida, Tsimshian, Tlingit, Nootka-Kwakiutl and Bellacoola). Like the other First Nations, the Salish favoured this region for its remarkably mild climate and abundance of orcas, salmon, seals, fruit and other resources. This beneficial environment, combined with the barrier formed by the nearby mountains, enabled the coastal tribes to thrive. Not only was their population quite large, but it was also significantly denser than that of other Aboriginal nations in central and eastern Canada.

In 1820, there were some 25,000 Salish living on the shores of the Fraser River, from its mouth south of Vancouver all the way up into the Rockies. Like other Aboriginal tribes, the Salish were sedentary and lived in villages of red cedar longhouses. They traded with other nations along the coast during

Portrait

potlatches, festive ceremonies lasting weeks on end and marked by the exchange of gifts.

Belated Exploration

The 18th century saw an increase in exploration and colonization all over the world as European sea powers scoured the planet hungering for natural riches and new territories. The African shores were well charted, and no stone had been left unturned on the east coast of North America. There was, however, an immense area that still seemed inaccessible: the far-off and mysterious Pacific Ocean. Some of the many peoples inhabiting its shores were completely unknown to French, Spanish and English navigators. The Panama Canal had not yet been dug, and sailing ships had to cover incredible distances, their crews braving starvation just to reach the largest of the Earth's oceans.

The voyages of French navigator Louis Antoine de Bougainville and English explorer James Cook, removed some of the mystery surrounding these distant lands. After Australia (1770) and New Zealand (1771), Cook explored the coast of British Columbia (1778). He did not, however, venture as far as the Strait of Georgia where Vancouver now lies.

In 1792, Cook's compatriot George Vancouver (1757-1798) became the first European to trod upon the soil that would give rise to the future city. He was on a mission to take possession of the territory for the King of England, and by so doing put an end to any plans the Russians and Spaniards had of laying claim to the region. The former would have liked to extend their empire southward from Alaska, while the latter were looking northward. From California, Spanish explorers had even made a brief trip into Burrard Inlet in the 16th century. This far-flung region was not coveted enough to cause any bloody wars, however, and was left undeveloped for years to come.

The Vancouver region was hard to reach not only by sea, but also by land with the virtually insurmountable obstacle of the Rocky

Mountains blocking the way. Imagine setting out across the immense North American continent from Montreal, following the lakes and rivers of the Canadian Shield, and exhausting yourself crossing the endless Prairies, only to end up barred from the Pacific by a wall of rock several thousand metres high. In 1908, the fabulously wealthy fur merchant and adventurer Simon Fraser became the first person to reach the site of Vancouver from inland. This belated breakthrough had little impact on the region, though, since Fraser was unable to reach any trade agreements with the coastal tribes and quickly withdrew to his trading posts in the Rockies.

The Salish Indians thus continued to lead a peaceful existence here for many more years before being disrupted by white settlers. In 1808, except for sporadic visits by Russians, Spaniards and Englishmen looking to trade pelts for fabrics and objects from the Orient, the Aboriginal peoples were still living according to the traditions handed down to them by their ancestors. In fact, European influence on their lifestyle remained negligible until the mid-19th century at which point colonization of the territory began slowly.

Development of Natural Resources

In 1818, Great Britain and the United States created the condominium of Oregon, a vast fur-trading zone along the Pacific bounded by California to the south and Alaska to the north. In so doing, these two countries excluded the Russians and the Spanish from this region once and for all. The employees of the North West Company, founded in Montreal in 1784, combed the valley of the Fraser River in search of furs. Not only did they encounter the coastal Indians, whose precious resources they were depleting, but they also had to adapt to the tumultuous waterways of the Rockies, which made travelling by canoe nearly impossible. In 1827, after the Hudson's Bay Company took over the North West Company, a large fur-trading post was founded in Fort Langley on the shores of the Fraser some 90km east of the present site of Vancouver that would remain untouched for several more decades.

The 49th parallel was designated the border between the United States and British North America in 1846, cutting the hunting territories in half and thereby putting a damper on the

Hudson's Bay Company's activities in the region. It wasn't until the gold rush of 1858 that the region experienced another era of prosperity. When nuggets of the precious metal were discovered in the bed of the Fraser upriver from Fort Langley, a frenzy broke out. In the space of two years, the valley of the golden river attracted thousands of prospectors, and makeshift wooden villages went up overnight. Some came from Eastern Canada, but most, including a large number of Chinese Americans, were from California.

In the end, however, it was contemporary industrialists' growing interest in the region's cedar and fir trees that led to the actual founding of Vancouver. In 1862, Sewell Prescott Moody, originally from Maine (U.S.), opened the region's first sawmill at the far end of Burrard Inlet, and ensured its success by creating an entire town, known as Moodyville, around it. A second sawmill, called Hastings Mills, opened east of present-day Chinatown in 1865. Two years later, innkeeper Gassy Jack Deighton arrived in the area and set up a saloon near Hastings Mills, providing a place for sawmill workers to slake their thirst. Before long, various service establishments sprang up around the saloon, thus marking the

birth of Gastown, later Vancouver's first neighbourhood.

In 1870, the colonial government of British Columbia renamed the nascent town Granville, after the Duke of Granville. The area continued to develop, and the city of Vancouver was officially founded in April 1886. It was renamed in honour of Captain George Vancouver who made the first hydrographic surveys of the shores of the Strait of Georgia. Unfortunately, a few weeks later, a forest fire swept through the new town, wiping out everything in its way. In barely 20 minutes, Vancouver was reduced to ashes. In those difficult years, local residents were still cut off from the rest of the world, so the town was reconstructed with an eye on the long term. From that point on, Vancouver's buildings, whether of wood or brick, were made to last.

The Umbilical Cord

The end of the gold rush in 1865 led to a number of economic problems for the colony of British Columbia. Due to American protectionism, local industrialists and merchants could not distribute their products in California, while Montreal was too far away and too hard to reach to be a lucrative market. The only favourable outlets, therefore, were the other British colonies on the Pacific, which paved the way for Vancouver's present prosperity. In 1871, British Columbia agreed to join the Canadian Confederation on the condition that a railway line linking it to the eastern part of the country be built.

Recognizing the potential of this gateway to the Pacific, a group of businessmen from Montreal set out to build a transcontinental railway in 1879. Angus, Allan, McIntyre, Strathcona (Smith), Stephen and the other men who joined forces under the Canadian Pacific banner were not thinking small; they wanted to transform Canada, theretofore only a nation in the political sense of the word, into an economically unified power. Canadian Pacific chose Port Moody (formerly Moodyville) as the western terminus of the railway. On July 4, 1886, the first train from Montreal reached Port Moody after a tortuous journey of about 5,000km. British Columbia was no longer cut off from the rest of the world; from that point on, it was regularly supplied with goods from Europe, Quebec and Ontario, and could export its own raw materials to more lucrative markets.

A few years later, the tracks were extended 20km to Vancouver in order to link the transcontinental railway to the new port and thereby allow greater access to the Asian market. This change proved momentous for the city whose population exploded from 2,500 inhabitants in 1886 to over 120,000 in 1911! Many of the Chinese who had come to North America to help build (and be exploited by) the railway settled in Vancouver when the project was finished, generating a certain degree of resentment among white residents who found the new immigrants a little too exotic for their liking. Nevertheless, the Chinese who had worked for Canadian Pacific and the gold mines in the Rockies were soon joined by Asians from Canton, Japan and Tonkin. The city's Chinatown, which grew up between Gastown and Hastings Mills, eventually became the second largest in North America after San Francisco's.

At the beginning of the 20th century, the city's economic activity gradually shifted from Gastown to the Canadian Pacific Railway yards, located around Granville Street. Within a few years, lovely stone buildings housing banks and department stores sprang up in this area. Nevertheless, most local residents still earned

Portrait

their livelihood from the lumber and fishing industries and lived in makeshift camps on the outskirts of town. In those days, therefore, downtown Vancouver's rapid development was to some extent artificial, based on visions of prosperity that would not be realized for some time yet. In 1913, the city was much like a gangling adolescent in the midst of a growth spurt. It was then that a major economic crisis occurred, putting an end to local optimism for a while. The opening of the Panama Canal (1914) and the end of World War I enabled Vancouver to emerge from this morass, only to sink right back into it during the crash of 1929. During World War II, residents of Japanese descent were interned and their possessions confiscated. Paranoia prevailed over reason, and these second- and sometimes even third-generation Vancouverites were viewed as potential spies.

The New Metropolis of the Pacific

As a result of the Canadian Pacific railway company's

strong presence on the West Coast, Vancouverites turned their attention away from the ocean stretched out before them and concentrated instead on their ties with central and eastern Canada. Nevertheless, the city's dual role as a gateway to the Pacific for North Americans and a gateway to America for Asians was already well established. This was shown by the massive influx of Chinese immigrants from the 19th century onwards and the numerous import-export businesses dealing in silk, tea and porcelain. The name Vancouver has thus been familiar throughout the Pacific zone for over a century. Starting in 1960, a decline in rail transport to the east prompted the city to shift its attention outward and concentrate on its role as a Pacific metropolis.

With the explosive economic growth of places like Japan, Hong Kong, Taiwan, Singapore, the Philippines, Malaysia and Thailand, especially in regards to exportation, Vancouver's port expanded at lightning speed. Since 1980, it has been the busiest one in the country. Vancouver's pleasant climate and stunning scenery attract large numbers of eastern Canadians looking to improve their quality of life as well as Asians seeking a new place to live and invest their money. For example, many affluent residents of Hong Kong, anxious about what would happen when their protectorate returned to China in 1997, chose to relocate here.

Thanks to all this new blood, Vancouver (especially the downtown core) has enjoyed continued growth since the late 1960s. Even more than San Francisco or Los Angeles, Vancouver has a strong, positive image throughout the Pacific. It is viewed as a neutral territory offering a good yield on investments and a comfortable standard of living.

The holding of the Asia-Pacific Economic (APEC) summit in Vancouver in November 1997 solidified Vancouver's position as a key player on the Pacific Rim, and should bolster its status in this market. APEC is a regional consultative body aimed at promoting open trade and economic cooperation between member countries. These include: Australia, Brunei, Canada, Chile, China, Hong Kong, Indonesia, Japan, South Korea, Malaysia, Mexico, New Zealand, Papua New Guinea, Philippines, Singapore, Taiwan, Thailand and the United States.

Population

Portrait

Vancouver has always been considered the "end of the line" in Canada, the final destination for those looking for a better world. From the era of the steamship, the transcontinental railroad to the modern age of the jumbo jet, the city has continued to attract adventurers eager to line their pockets as well as more philosophical souls looking for peace and a sense of well-being. Located at the edge of a continent that developed from east to west, Vancouver was shrouded in mystery for many years, a sort of Eldorado tinged with Confucianism from the far reaches of the world. These two visions of Vancouver sometimes lead to confrontations between people concerned primarily with economics and developing natural resources and those more interested in ecology. In the end, though, everyone agrees and revels in Vancouver's west-coast way of life.

In 1989, there were 1,471,844 people living in Greater Vancouver; today, there are an estimated 1,830,000. The population has thus grown 14% over the past seven years, illustrating the city's economic vitality and the continued attraction it holds for newcomers. In 1999, the population reached two million. Even early on, Vancouver had a multi-ethnic population. In the wake of the colonial era, however, residents of British descent still formed a large majority. A number of Americans came here during the gold rush. Soon after, the first wave of Chinese immigrants established the city's Chinatown which grew considerably after the completion of the Canadian Pacific railway (1886), a good part of which was built by Asian labourers. Before long, a Japanese community was born, further diversifying the city's "Pacific" profile. Today, Vancouver has over 200,000 residents of Asian descent.

The city's cultural mosaic became that much richer in the 20th century when immigrants from Europe (especially Germany, Poland, Italy and Greece) began arriving. In 1989, Vancouverites of British descent made up only about 30% of the total population. The French Canadian population, which has always been small in British Columbia, stands at about 29,000 (1986), while the aboriginal population has dwindled to 12,000 (1991).

Culture

Vancouver's reputation has long been one of a very laid-back city whose beautiful landscape is linked to the "coolness" of its inhabitants living in communion with nature. Started in 1920, the Polar Bear Swim, an annual dip in the cold waters of English Bay on New Year's Day, became one of the rare "sociocultural" events. At the time, skiing, hiking and boating were a part of everyday life and cultural life was practically nonexistent. People living in small communities in the area reserved their Sundays for hockey or baseball.

Sports are now at the heart of some very outstanding events in Vancouver. Fans devote particular energy to the cause. Spectators at state-of-the-art GM Place stadium and patrons of bars with giant television screens drink beer and munch on spicy chicken wings. On June 14, 1994, when the Vancouver Canucks took part in the Stanley Cup finals, 70,000 people flooded Robson Street and there was even a riot.

With an economy based primarily on lumber and fishing, the city lived essentially self-sufficiently until Expo '86 took place there in 1986 and had a significant effect on Vancouver's economy and reputation. Previously unknown on the world stage, the city started to attract tourists and investors, especially from Asia. In response to this economic revival, sky-scrapers started popping up that competed in height with the magnificent Art-Deco-style Marine Building and the majestic Hotel Vancouver, built around the same time. Consequently, Vancouver has put a lot of emphasis on architecture. Its most recent addition, the new municipal library, is highly characteristic of the work of its designer, Moshe Safdi. In shape and colour, it is reminiscent of the Roman Coliseum ruins. Tourism has also experienced a lot of growth since Expo '86 and has become an important source of revenue for Vancouver. Cruises to Alaska are one successful example of the city's efforts to develop its tourist industry.

Vancouver's gay community – the largest in Canada – has grown over the years and its vibrancy contributes greatly to making the city more exciting. Many groups have been founded for the purpose of promoting human rights. In terms of culture, the gay community here is very active and heavily involved in the fields of classical music, singing and visual arts.

Marker for Change

To commemorate the killing of 14 women at the École Polytechnique in Montréal in 1989, the Women's Monument Committee erected the Marker for Change on December 6, 1997, the eighth anniversary of the massacre. Designed by Torontonian Beth Alber, it features 14 pink-granite benches, each inscribed with the name of one of the victims, that form a circle in Thornton Park in East Vancouver. The monument's dedication in hommage to all women killed by men is in seven languages.

Because of its geographic location, Vancouver has always been an inspiration to artists. But artistic and cultural activity here has only really started to develop in the last two decades and is slowly becoming more established. Emily Carr (1871-1945), with her relentless desire to depict the natural environment of this isolated area, at a time when there were no means of transportation, was the most striking and encouraging role model for artists who followed. Her paintings are in all of Vancouver's museums along with works by members of the Group of Seven who made landscapes throughout Canada famous. Aboriginal art is highly prominent in the area and its two most important representatives are Robert Davidson and, especially, the great sculptor, Bill Reid.

The mixture of various ethnic backgrounds gives Vancouver a distinctive character. The diversity of customs and beliefs is starting to interest more people. Fashion shows and exhibitions are on the rise. Also, Asian immigration brings considerable cultural and economic dynamism. Communities from mainland China, Hong Kong and Taiwan preserve their cultures which are rich in symbols and events. The Dragon Boat Festival and Chinese New Year are the biggest events during which Vancouver becomes immersed in Chinese culture for many days.

Cinema has always been a part of daily life in Vancouver. A day doesn't go by when there isn't a film crew on one of Vancouver's streets. Studios have been established in North Vancouver and it's no longer surprising to run into Hollywood stars on the streets or in the shops. Every autumn, the Vancouver International Film Festival offers close to 150 quality foreign films, much to the pleasure of film buffs.   Since 1997, the film festivals have been multiplying. The largest ones are devoted to European countries, such as France. Vancouver has a fertile film industry and there's always an excellent selection of French, Italian and Japanese movies. British Columbian producers and local talents are also starting to emerge.

The fireworks festival sponsored by Benson & Hedges is a sacred summer ritual. Every year, at the end of July, over 200,000 people serenely make their way to the beaches on English Bay to attend four extraordinary pyrotechnic performances.

Theatre and music are experiencing exceptional growth, internationally reputed artists, such as Pavarotti, Céline Dion and Cher, perform here regularly. Their many incarnations offer wonderful opportunities and create the best conditions for both artists and fans.

Visual artists here are increasingly coming to the fore while the Vancouver Art Gallery exhibits are becoming more interesting every year. The exposition devoted to Picasso's drawings and Toulouse-Lautrec's advertisements demonstrate an artistic initiative that is constantly expanding its horizons.

All levels of society support the visual arts, and schools and libraries exhibit local artists' work. The arts in Vancouver are a reflection of the cultural diversity of its population and the West Coast spirit. The performing arts have two brand new theatres, and literature and dance are also flourishing.

The multicultural influence is striking, and each culture expresses itself and blossoms in this environment. The city of Vancouver also offers an impressive array of cultural attractions: a traditional Chinese garden, Greek, Chinese and Japanese cultural festivals, a classical ballet, a Chinese opera, Sumo shows, a Welsh choir, a baroque orchestra, jazz and blues as well as statues depicting modern and Aboriginal sculptures. For information on the artistic activities in Vancouver, call the Arts Hotline at ☎684-ARTS (☎684-2787).

Vancouver is also favoured among writers for the Vancou-ver Writers Festival which organized over 40 events last year.

The city is also slowly starting to gain recognition for its many fine restaurants, which are often influenced by various types of international cuisine and offer the added touch of friendly service. Viticulture, or wine growing, is in full expansion. Wine festivals abound with consumers' tastes becoming more refined. This cultural explosion, reaching beyond the borders of British Columbia and even Canada, has been so successful that important summits, such as the one between Clinton and Yeltsin, have taken place here over recent years.

Famous Vancouverites

Vancouver boasts an increasing number of world-famous personalities, particularly in the world of film. Its climate and natural environment, and fiscal conditions attractive to American producers have contributed to making such Canadian actors as **Cameron Bancroff, Margot Kidder, Michael J. Fox, Bruce Greenwood** and **Cynthia Stevenson** known to the public. American stars such as **Christopher Reeve**, who starred in *Super-*

man, **Mel Gibson**, featured in *Bird On A Wire*, which was shot in the streets of Gastown, and **Jackie Chan**, who shook the downtown area in *Rumble in the Bronx*, have also been captivated by Vancouver's charm. The list hardly ends here. **Robert DeNiro, Goldie Hawn, Charlton Heston** and many others have shot movies in the streets of Vancouver. Moreover, until recently, *The X Files* was a "made in Vancouver" production. Another anecdote: blond bombshell **Pamela Anderson** is also from Vancouver.

Bryan Adams

This rock superstar has sold over 45 million records throughout the world. He comes from West Vancouver where he still has a house. He returns occasionally to record songs and sign autographs.

Joe Average

He is a contemporary figurative artist, using bright colours in his work. His posters can be seen throughout the city; one of these was used as official promotion for the International Conference on AIDS. He decided to dedicate his art to the cause of AIDS upon being diagnosed as HIV positive.

Squire Barnes

He has been a sports commentator (especially for hockey) on CBC television for more than 10 years. The province's best known, popular and lively announcer, he's a down-to-earth, straightforward guy who performs his job with precision and a sense of humour. He also writes for some sports magazines. In 1998, he received the Orange prize awarded to the liveliest person on television.

Dave Barr

This Vancouver golfer has been taking part in international tournaments for 20 years. Born in Kelowna, in the Okanagan Valley, he began his career in 1974 and has represented Canada 13 times at the World Cup, winning it twice.

Niels Bendtsen

Another famous Vancouverite, Niels Bendtsen is a furniture designer whose art has transcended national boundaries. His work is on permanent display at the New York Museum of Modern Art, and his output extends all the way to Europe. Closer to home, he designed the interior layout of the Starbucks coffee shops.

George Bowering

This major literary personality from Vancouver became famous in the sixties as the founder and editor in chief of *Tish* magazine. His reputation has been growing ever since. An English professor at SFU, he has written and published over 40 books of poetry, fiction and history, and has received the Governor General's Award on three occasions.

Jay Brazeau

This Vancouver actor attracted notice in the well-known television series *We're No Angels* and *The X Files*. He has also worked in radio and received three Jessie Awards. Leading actor in the recent film *Kissed*, he remains part of the current film scene.

Kim Campbell

She was Canada's first female Prime Minister, but was not re-elected. In 1996, she was named Consul-General of Canada in Los Angeles.

James Cheng

A very wealthy architect born in Hong Kong, he has become the darling of Vancouver. He is currently focusing on the construction of large buildings, giving precedence to quality of life and the environment.

Douglas Coupland

The man who coined the term "Generation X" is another famous Vancouverite. He currently lives on the side of the North Shore Mountains and resurfaces every now and then to put in his two cents worth on the future of Canada, British Columbia and of course Vancouver. He stresses the idea that Vancouver's geography alone distinguishes it tremendously from the rest of Canada, and that it is developing an identity quite apart from the other major Canadian cities (see also p 195).

Sam Feldman

Through his dynamism, will and talent as a talent agent, he is now involved in all North American musical productions and film scores. He represents 150 artists, including Bryan Adams.

Jim Pattison

Jim Pattison is without a doubt the most powerful and respected businessman in Vancouver. He is also the wealthiest. His companies employ 17,000 people and make between three and

Portrait

four billion dollars in annual sales.

Sarah McLachlan

Born in Halifax, Nova Scotia, Sarah McLachlan nevertheless considers herself a Vancouver artist. It may have something to do with the fact that her record label is the Vancouver-based Nettwerk. Fans appreciate her ethereal voice and emotional and forthright songs. Her latest album, *Surfacing*, is already a success. Lilith Fair, the all-female musical tour conceived by McLachlan that she claims "*doesn't exclude men*" but "*simply celebrates women*," has made her one of the most well-known female performers in North America. Sarah McLaughlan's singing career, as well as the lawsuit filled against her by a composer, have made her doubly famous in Vancouver. For the past two years, she's had the top selling albums in western Canada.

Mark Messier

He's the most valuable player on the Vancouver Canucks hockey team. At 38 years old, after playing for the Edmonton Oilers and the New York Rangers for most of his career, he has a total of 18 years in the limelight. He has scored more than 600 goals during his career playing centre. There is a chance, however, that Messier could soon be traded to another team.

Jason Priestley

This young actor from U.S. television and film is Vancouver's darling child. His success in Beverly Hills 90210 quickly made him a celebrity. He is often invited to major events in the province that are occasions for him to come home and visit his family.

Bill Reid

Established in Vancouver, this great sculptor has represented the art of his Haida ancestors with much influence and skill since 1940. His sculptures can be seen all over the city as well as at the UBC Museum of Anthropology and the Vancouver Art Gallery. Two of his works not be missed are the one at the Aquarium and the magnificent sculpture at the Vancouver airport. Reid died in March 1998.

Paul Watson

Co-founder of Greenpeace, he is now president of the Sea Shepherd Conservation Society which protects the environment and, particularly the waters and their fauna. He has often come under criticism, with some comparing his methods to those of an "eco-terrorist."

Architecture

Vancouver was founded during an era of eager westward expansion. Within a few months in 1865, scores of wooden buildings sprang up here, providing the employees of the area's newly opened sawmills with places to sleep, purchase goods and entertain themselves. The vast majority of these makeshift structures fell victim either to the wear and tear of time or the devastating fire of 1886 that destroyed a large part of the young city. You can see one of the few buildings that has survived from that era in Pioneer Park (see p 108).

In the years following the fire, the centre of town, located in what is now Gastown, was reconstructed out of brick to prevent destruction of the growing city by another blaze. The earliest buildings of that era were modelled after the Italianate architecture that had enjoyed such great popularity on the east coast two decades prior (prominent cornices, small pediments over doors and windows). But Vancouver caught up quickly, adopting Richardson's neo-Roman-

esque style, as other cities all over North America had done. This style, inspired by French Romanesque art, was reinterpreted by Boston architect Henry Hobson Richardson who designed massive, robust-looking structures with large, arched openings. Other late 19th-century buildings have more in common with the vernacular architecture of San Francisco (multi-level oriel windows overhanging sidewalks, projecting cornices) that are evidence of Vancouver's close ties with the rest of the west coast.

At the beginning of the 20th century, Vancouver experienced a period of phenomenal growth. Entire neighbourhoods sprang up in a single summer. In most residential areas, wood was the material of choice, since it was inexpensive and available in large quantities. The risks of fire, furthermore, were minimal as the houses were almost all freestanding. Space was not a problem, so San Francisco's Queen Anne style, characterized by numerous gables and turrets, was used for these homes. Downtown, brick slowly gave way to stone, a richer material, since proud Vancouverites were eager to show the rest of the world that they were dynamic and urbane. It is for that reason that the largest skyscraper in the British Empire (see Sun Tower,

Portrait

p 68) was built in Vancouver, rather than in Toronto or London, in 1912. Next, Canadian Pacific introduced the Château style to Vancouver, along with the Beaux-Arts style and its offshoots, neo-Classical revival and baroque revival, which are all well represented here. The Chinese community also made a significant contribution to the city's architecture, building narrow commercial buildings with deep loggias and parapets on top, reflecting an interesting blend of North American and Asian styles.

Starting in 1913, Vancouver experienced a growth slump from which it did not truly recover until after the Second World War. Consequently, few new buildings went up in the twenties and thirties. You will nevertheless find a few examples of the Art Deco style here, including the Marine Building which faces straight down West Hastings Street (see p 74). It is viewed as one of the landmarks of the business district.

As Vancouver is a thriving young city, its architecture is predominantly modern and post-modern. Thanks to talented architects who are open to experimentation and a cultural climate that combines innovative Californian influences with the traditional building techniques of China, Japan and even some of British Columbia's Aboriginal communities, the city has developed an exceptional and modern architectural heritage since the 1940s.

From the glass and steel skyscrapers downtown to the houses clinging to mountainsides in North and West Vancouver, with their simple post-and-beam construction, the accent is usually on purity of line. This sober, sophisticated style contrasts sharply with the ostentation of the early part of the century... and to a certain extent that of contemporary, late 20th-century architecture as well. Indeed, since the emergence of post-modernism, there has been a shift back to the lavish forms of the past. Many recent immigrants favour columns and decorated pediments which they proudly photograph for their families back home. In some areas, furthermore, houses built in the fifties and sixties are being replaced by what Vancouverites have termed "monster-houses"; giant structures that take up almost their entire plot of land, usurping space once occupied by trees and gardens.

Practical Information

Information in this chapter will help visitors better plan their trip to Vancouver.

Entrance Formalities

Passport

For a stay of less than three months in Canada, a valid passport is usually sufficient for most visitors and a visa is not required. American residents do not need passports, though these are the best form of identification. A three-month extension is possible, but a return ticket and proof of sufficient funds to cover this extension may be required.

Caution: some countries do not have an agreement with Canada concerning health and accident insurance, so it is advisable to have the appropriate coverage. For more information, see the section entitled, "Health," on page 49.

Canadian citizens who wish to enter the United States, to visit Alaska or Washing-

ton State for example, do not need visas; neither do citizens of the majority of Western European countries. A valid passport is sufficient for a stay of less than three months. A return ticket and proof of sufficient funds to cover your stay may be required.

Extended Visits

A visitor must submit a request to extend his or her visit **in writing, before** the expiration of his or her visa (the date is usually written in your passport) to an Immigration Canada office. To make a request you must have a valid passport, a return ticket, proof of sufficient funds to cover the stay as well as the $65 non-refundable filing-fee. In some cases (work, study), however, the request must be made **before** arriving in Canada.

Customs

If you are bringing gifts into Canada, remember that certain restrictions apply.

Smokers (minimum age is 16 to smoke, 19 to buy) can bring in a maximum of 200 cigarettes, 50 cigars, 400 grams of tobacco, or 400 tobacco sticks.

For wine and alcohol the limit is 1.1 litres; in practice, however, two bottles per person are usually allowed. The limit for beer is 24 355ml size cans or bottles.

Plants, vegetation, and food: there are very strict rules regarding the importation of plants, flowers, and other vegetation; it is therefore not advisable to bring any of these types of products into the country. If it is absolutely necessary, contact the Customs-Agriculture service of the Canadian embassy **before** leaving your country.

Pets: if you are travelling with your pet, you will need a health certificate (available from your veterinarian) as well as a rabies vaccination certificate. It is important to remember that the vaccination must have been administered **at least 30 days before** your departure and should not be more than a year old.

Tax reimbursements for visitors: it is possible to be reimbursed for certain taxes paid on purchases made in Canada (see p 57).

Embassies and Consulates

Canadian Embassies and Consulates Abroad

AUSTRALIA
Canadian Consulate General
Level 5, Quay West
111 Harrington Road
Sydney, N.S.W., Australia 2000
☎*(612) 364-3000*
⇌*(612) 364-3098*

BELGIUM
Canadian Embassy
2 Avenue de Tervueren
1040 Brussels
☎*735.60.40*
⇄*732.67.90*

DENMARK
Canadian Embassy
Kr. Bernikowsgade 1
DK=1105 Copenhagen K
☎*12.22.99*
⇄*14.05.85*

FINLAND
Canadian Embassy
Pohjos Esplanadi 25 B
00100 Helsinki
☎*171-141*
⇄*601-060*

GERMANY
Canadian Consulate General
Internationales
Handelzentrum
Friedrichstrasse 95, 23rd Floor
10117 Berlin
☎*261.11.61*
⇄*262.92.06*

GREAT BRITAIN
Canada High Commission
Macdonald House
One Grosvenor Square
London W1X 0AB
☎*258-6600*
⇄*258-6384*

ITALY
Canadian Embassy
Via G.B. de Rossi 27
00161 Rome
☎*44.59.81*
⇄*44.59.87*

NETHERLANDS
Canadian Embassy
Parkstraat 25
2514JD The Hague
☎*361-4111*
⇄*365-6283*

NORWAY
Canadian Embassy
Oscars Gate 20
Oslo 3
☎*46.69.55*
⇄*69.34.67*

SPAIN
Canadian Embassy
Edificio Goya
Calle Nunez de Balboa 35
28001 Madrid
☎*431.43.00*
⇄*431.23.67*

SWEDEN
Canadian Embassy
Tegelbacken 4, Seventh floor
Stockholm
☎*613-9900*
⇄*24.24.91*

SWITZERLAND
Canadian Embassy
Kirchenfeldstrasse 88
3000 Berne 6
☎*532.63.81*
⇄*352.73.15*

UNITED STATES
Canadian Embassy
501 Pennsylvania Avenue NW
Washington, DC, 20001
☎*(202) 682-1740*
⇄*(202) 682-7726*

Practical
Information

Canadian Consulate General
Suite 400 South Tower
One CNN Center
Atlanta, Georgia, 30303-2705
☎ *(404) 577-6810 or 577-1512*
⇌ *(404) 524-5046*

Canadian Consulate General
Three Copley Place, Suite 400
Boston, Massachusetts, 02116
☎ *(617) 262-3760*
⇌ *(617) 262-3415*

Canadian Consulate General
Two Prudential Plaza
180 North Stetson Avenue, Suite 2400
Chicago, Illinois, 60601
☎ *(312) 616-1860*
⇌ *(312) 616-1877*

Canadian Consulate General
St. Paul Place, Suite 1700
750 North St. Paul Street
Dallas, Texas, 75201
☎ *(214) 922-9806*
⇌ *(214) 922-9815*

Canadian Consulate General
600 Renaissance Center, Suite 1100
Detroit, Michigan, 48234-1798
☎ *(313) 567-2085*
⇌ *(313) 567-2164*

Canadian Consulate General
300 South Grande Avenue
10th Floor, California Plaza
Los Angeles, California, 90071
☎ *(213) 687-7432*
⇌ *(213) 620-8827*

Canadian Consulate General
Suite 900
701 Fourth Avenue South
Minneapolis, Minnesota, 55415-1899
☎ *(612) 333-4641*
⇌ *(612) 332-4061*

Canadian Consulate General
1251 Avenue of the Americas
New York, New York, 10020-1175
☎ *(212) 596-1600*
⇌ *(212) 596-1793*

Canadian Consulate General
One Marine Midland Center
Suite 3000
Buffalo, New York, 14203-2884
☎ *(716) 852-1247*
⇌ *(716) 852-4340*

Canadian Consulate General
412 Plaza 600
Sixth and Stewart Streets
Seattle, Washington, 98101-1286
☎ *(206) 442-1777*
⇌ *(206) 443-1782*

Foreign Consulates in Vancouver

Australian Consulate
888 Dunsmuir
Suite 1225
Vancouver, BC, V6C 3K4
☎ *(604) 684-1177*
⇌ *(604) 684-1856*

Honorary Consulate of Belgium
Mon to Wed 9am to noon
Birks Place, Suite 570
688 West Hastings
Vancouver, BC, V6B 1P4
☎ *(604) 684-6838*

British Consulate General
1111 Melville St., Suite 800
Vancouver, BC, V6E 3V6
☎ *(604) 683-4421*

Consulate General of Germany
Mon to Fri 9am to noon
World Trade Centre
999 Canada Place, Suite 704
Vancouver, BC, V6C 3E1
☎*(604) 684-8377*
(604) 684-8334

Consulate General of Italy
Mon to Fri 9am to 12:30pm,
Wed 3pm to 5pm
1200 Burrard Street, Suite 705
Vancouver, B.C., V6Z 2C7
☎*684-7288*
685-4263

**Consulate General
of the Netherlands**
Mon to Fri 9:15am to
12:15pm, closed Wed
475 Howe Street, Suite 821
Vancouver, BC, V6C 2B3
☎*(604) 684-6448*
(604) 684-3549

Consulate General of Spain
9198 Primula Pl.
Burnaby, BC, V3N 4W8
☎*(604) 520-6222*
There is no Spanish consulate in Vancouver. If you have any inquiries, contact the consulate general in Burnaby.

or in Toronto:
1200 Bay Street, Suite 400
Toronto, ON, M5R 2A5
☎*(416) 977-1661*
(416) 925-4949

**Consulate General
of Switzerland**
999 Canada Place, Suite 790
Vancouver, BC, V6C 3E1
☎*(604) 684-2231*
(604) 684-2806

U.S. Consulate General
1095 West Pender
Vancouver, BC, V6E 2M6
☎*(604) 685-4311*
(604) 685-7175

Tourist Information

The **area code** is *604*, unless otherwise indicated.

Vancouver Tourist Info Centre
May to Sep, every day 8am to
6pm; Sep to May, Mon to Fri
8:30am to 5pm, Sat 9am to
5pm
Plaza Level, Waterfront Centre
200 Burrard St., V6C 3L6
☎*683-2000*
682-6839
www.tourism-vancouver.org
provides brochures and information on sights and accommodations for the city as well as for the province.

**Super, Natural
British Columbia**
☎*800-663-6000*

or write to them at:
Box 9830,Station Province-Government, Victoria, V8W 9W5
For information on and reservations for travelling in the rest of the province you can call:

Vancouver Parks & Recreation
☎*257-8400*
Provides all information on sports and recreation activities.

Calendar of Sports and Cultural Events
24hrs/day
☎*661-7373*

For information on Vancouver and British Columbia on the internet, check out the following sites:

Tourism Vancouver
☎*683-2000*
www.tourism-vancouver.org

In Vancouver!
www.vancouver-bc.com

Excite Travel
www.city.net/countries/canada/british_columbia/

Super, Natural British Columbia
www.travel.bc.ca

Canada Tourism Commission
62-65 Trafalgar Square
London WC2N 5DT
public enquiries
☎*0891 715000*
(premium rate)
⇌*0171 389 1149*
e-mail vcc@dial.pipex.com
can provide general tourist information for the whole country.

Guided Tours

Guided tours of all sorts are available to help you discover every facet of Vancouver.

Gastown Business Improvement Society
131 Water St.
☎*683-5650*
offers free walking tours of Gastown once a day during the months of June, July and August. Tours last about 2hrs.

Gray Line of Vancouver
255 First Ave. E.
☎*879-3363 or 800-667-0882*
offers city tours year-round aboard comfortable buses. The tour lasts 3.5hrs and costs $40 for adults and $28 for children. In the summer, they also offer a shorter double-decker tour. You can get on and off as you please; the cost for a two-day pass is $24 for adults and $13 for children. The route is posted in the lobbies of most downtown hotels and the entire tour takes about 2hrs. You must purchase your ticket ahead of time, either by calling the above numbers or by visiting the agent in the lobby of the Hotel Vancouver (see p 140). Gray Line also offers excursions to Victoria and Whistler.

The Vancouver Trolley Company Ltd.
875 Terminal Ave.
☎*801-5515 or 888-451-5581*
toots around town in a old-fashioned trolleys, picking up and dropping off passengers as they wish at 16 different stops, and providing narration the whole way.

Harbour Cruises Ltd.
☎*688-7246 or 800-663-1500*
organizes narrated boat
tours of the Inner Harbour
that last about 90min and
departs three times daily at
11:30am, 1pm and 2:30pm.
The cost is $18 for adults
and $6 for children. They
also offer sunset dinner
cruises which feature a buffet meal and a trip out to
English Bay and False
Creek. This is a great way
to experience this city set
between sea and sky.

**Stanley Park
Horse Drawn Tours**
☎*681-5115*
≈*681-5116*
Stanley Park Horse Drawn
Tours offers 1hr-long jaunts
through beautiful Stanley
Park. Your carriage awaits
at the information booth at
the Coal harbour parking
lot every day from mid-
March to November. There
are departures every 20 to
30min and the cost is $15
for adults and $10 for chil-
dren.

**West Coast City and Nature
Sightseeing Tours**
$39-$99
3945 Myrtle St., Burnaby, BC
☎*451-1600*
has multilingual guides and
offers minibus tours year
round. Destinations include
Whistler, Victoria, Capilano
and Butchart Gardens.

Getting There

By Plane

From Europe

There are two possibilities:
direct flights or flights with
a stopover in Montreal,
Toronto or Calgary. Direct
flights are of course much
more attractive since they
are considerably faster than
flights with a stopover (for
example expect about 9hrs
from Amsterdam for a direct
flight compared to 13hrs).
In some cases, however,
particularly if you have a lot
of time, it can be advantageous to combine a charter
flight from Europe with one
of the many charter flights
within Canada from either
Montreal or Toronto. Prices
for this option can vary
considerably depending on
whether you are travelling
during high or low season.

At press time, five airline
companies offered direct
flights from Europe to Vancouver.

Air Canada offers daily direct
flights during the summer
from Paris to Vancouver
and from London to Van-
couver. Air Canada also
flies twice a week from
Frankfurt to Vancouver.

*Practical
Information*

Airlines
(information and reservations)

Air Canada and Canadian Airlines:	☎800-361-8620
Air China:	☎688-5515
Air France:	☎800-667-2747
American Airlines:	☎800-433-7300
Continental Airlines:	☎800-231-0856
Delta Airlines:	☎800-221-1212
Harbour Air:	☎688-1277
Horizon Air:	☎800-547-9308
Japan Airlines:	☎800-525-3663
KLM Royal Dutch:	☎279-5433
Lufthansa German Airline:	☎800-563-5459
Quantas Airways:	☎800-227-4500
United Airlines:	☎800-241-6522

Canadian Airlines offers direct flights from London to Vancouver, as well as direct flights from Frankfurt to Vancouver.

One should take note that the recent merger of these two airlines may affect flight schedules in the future.

KLM offers a direct flight from Amsterdam to Vancouver three times a week.

Lufthansa offers a daily flight in partnership with Canadian Airlines from Frankfurt to Vancouver.

British Airways offers daily non-stop service from London to Vancouver.

From the United States

Travellers arriving from the southern or southeastern United States may want to consider **American Airlines** which flies into Vancouver through Dallas.

Delta Airlines offers direct flights from Los Angeles to Vancouver. Travellers from the eastern United States go through Salt Lake City.

Northwest Airlines flies into Vancouver via Minneapolis.

From Asia

Both **Air Canada** and **Canadian Airlines** offer direct flights between Vancouver and Hong Kong.

Within Canada

Air Canada and **Canadian Airlines** are the only companies that offer regular flights to Vancouver within Canada. Daily flights to Vancouver as well as many other cities are offered from all the major cities in the country. Flights from Eastern Canada often have stopovers in Montreal or Toronto. For example Air Canada flies to Vancouver 14 times a week. During the high season, the aforementioned flights are complemented by many others offered by charter companies, including Air Transat, Royal and Canada 3000. These flights are subject to change with respect to availability and fares.

Air Canada's regional partner **Air BC** offers flights within British Columbia, as does Canadian Airlines' regional partner, **Canadian Regional**.

Harbour Air Seaplanes
☎ *688-1277 or 800-665-0212*
☎ *250-385-2203 in Victoria*
⇄ *278-5271*
offers scheduled flights to Victoria, the Gulf Islands and northern British Columbia.

Helijet Airways
☎ *273-1414 or 800-665-4354*
⇄ *688-4636*
provides scheduled helicopter service to Victoria and Seattle.

Airport

Vancouver International Airport
☎ *276-6101*
is served by flights from across Canada, the United States, Europe and Asia. Nineteen airline companies presently use the airport. The airport is located 15km from downtown.

It takes about 30min to get downtown by car or bus. A taxi or limousine will cost you about $25-$30, or you can take the **Airporter** bus (☎ *946-8866*) which offers shuttle service to the major downtown hotels and the bus depot. The cost is $10 one-way or $17 return for adults. The bus leaves every 15min and runs from 6:30am to 12:10am. To reach downtown by public transit take bus #100 for downtown and points east and bus #404 or #406 for Richmond, Delta and points south. The fare ranges from $1.75 and $3.50 depending on the time of day and destination.

Air Limo
☎273-1331
limousine to the airport: $29 20 to 40min journey time.

Take note: even if you have already paid various taxes included in the purchase price of your ticket, Vancouver International Airport charges every passenger an **Airport Improvement Fee** (AIF). The fee is $5 for flights within B.C. and to the Yukon, $10 for flights elsewhere in North America, and $15 for overseas flights; credit cards are accepted, and most in-transit passengers are exempted.

Besides the regular airport services (duty-free shops, cafeterias, restaurants), you will also find an exchange office. Several car rental companies also have offices in the airport, including Avis, Thrifty, ABC Rent-a-Car, Budget (see p 46).

By Train

Travellers with a lot of time may want to consider the train, one of the most pleasant and impressive ways to discover Western Canada and reach Vancouver. Via Rail Canada is the only company that offers train

travel between the Canadian provinces. This mode of transportation can be combined with air travel (various packages are offered by Air Canada and Canadian Airlines) or on its own from big cities in Eastern Canada like Toronto or Montreal. This last option does require a lot of time. However, it takes a minimum of five days to get from Montreal to Vancouver.

The **CanRailpass** is another particularly interesting option. Besides the advantageous price, you only need to purchase one ticket for travel throughout Canada. The ticket allows 12 days of unlimited travel in a 30-day period. At press-time the CanRailpass was $589 ($545 for children, seniors and students) in the high season and $379 ($355 for children, seniors and students) in the low season (Jan 1 to May 31 and Oct 16 to Dec 31). CanRailpass holders are also entitled to special rates for car rentals.

Via Rail offers several discounts:

Reductions for certain days of the week, during the off-season and on reservations made at least five days in advance: up to 40% off depending on the destination;

Discount for students and those 24 years of age or less: 10% throughout the year or 40% if the reservation is made five days in advance, except during the holidays;

Discount for people aged 60 and over: 10% on certain days during off-peak travel times;

Special rates for children: children two to 11 travel for half-price; children under two accompanied by an adult travel free;

Finally, take note that first-class service is quite exceptional, including a meal, wine, and alcoholic beverages free of charge.

For further information on Via trains:

www.viarail.ca

In Canada
☎*800-561-8630*
or contact your travel agent

In Australia
☎*(02) 9319 6624*
⇌*(02) 9318 2753*

In Italy
Gastaldi Tours
☎*(10) 59 991*
⇌*(10) 28 0354*

In the Netherlands
Incento B.V.
☎*(035) 69 55111*
⇌*(035) 69 55155*

In New Zealand
Walshes World
☎*(09) 379-3708*
⇌*(09) 309 0725*

In Switzerland
Touring Club Suisse
☎*(22) 737 1313*
⇌*(22) 737 1590*

In the United Kingdom
Leisurail
☎*0870 7500-222*
⇌*01733-505-451*

or Airsavers
☎*0141-303-0308*
⇌*041-303-0306*

In the United States
☎*800-561-3949*
or contact Amtrak or your travel agent.

Trains from the United States and eastern Canada arrive at the new intermodal **Pacific Central Station** *(Via Rail Canada, 1150 Station St.,* ☎*800-561-8630)* where you can also connect to buses or the surface public transportation system known as the **Skytrain**. The cross-country Via train, **The Canadian**, arrives in Vancouver three times a week from Eastern Canada. The trip from Edmonton to Vancouver is a spectacular trip through the mountains along the rivers and valleys. Those in a rush should keep in mind that the trip takes 24hrs, and is more of a tourist excursion than a means of transportation. It costs less than $200 one-way; check with Via, however, about seasonal rates.

BC Rail
1311 West First St., North Vancouver
☎**984-5246**
trains travel the northern west coast. Schedules vary depending on the seasons.

During the summer, the **Great Canadian Railtour Company Ltd.** offers **Rocky Mountain Railtours** *($725 per person, $670 per person double occupancy;* ☎*606-7200 or 800-665-7245, ≈606-7520)* between Calgary and Vancouver.

There is daily service aboard **Amtrak's Mount Baker International** from Seattle, Washington; the trip takes 3hrs and follows a scenic route. For reservations or information, call Amtrak US Rail at 800-USA-RAIL or 800-872-7245 (toll-free in North America).

Train Rides

The railway enabled Vancouver to open up to the rest of Canada. Due to the province's very steep terrain, some routes are still considered reckless, defying the very laws of engineering. These first-class local trains still run, travelling to regions and **landscapes** that would otherwise be inaccessible. All departures from Vancouver.

Royal Hudson
1311 West First St., North Vancouver
☎*631-3500*
The steam locomotive is very well-known in Vancouver tourist circles. Dating from the beginning of the century, but restored, it takes passengers from its station in North Vancouver to Squamish, 65km away. The journey allows passengers to discover the splendid **Howe Sound** fjord, as the railway skirts the shore.

Rocky Mountain Railtours
1150 Station St., Vancouver
☎*606-7200*
This agency's very comfortable train with vast carriages offering panoramic views will take you to the **Rockies** for several days. An extraordinary experience.

VIA Rail Canada
☎*800-561-8630*
For more information on railways radiating around Vancouver.

By Ferry

Two ferry ports serve the greater Vancouver area for travellers coming from other regions in the province. Horseshoe Bay, to the northwest, is the terminal for ferries to Nanaimo (crossing time 90min), Bowen Island and the Sunshine Coast. Tsawwassen, to the south, is the terminal for ferries to

Table of distances (km)
Via the shortest route

	Calgary (Alberta)	Edmonton (Alberta)	Harrison Hot Springs (B.C.)	Jasper (Alberta)	Seattle (Washington)	Vancouver (B.C.)
Edmonton (Alberta)	278					
Harrison Hot Springs (B.C.)	869	1147				
Jasper (Alberta)	408	365	893			
Seattle (Washington)	1086	1364	247	1128		
Vancouver (B.C.)	967	1155	125	794	226	
Whistler (B.C.)	907	1186	256	949	350	123

Example : The distance between Edmonton and Vancouver is 1155km.

© ULYSSES

Victoria (Swartz Bay) (crossing time 95min), Nanaimo (crossing time two hrs) and the Southern Gulf Islands. Both terminals are about 30min from downtown. For information on these routes, contact the **BC Ferries** (☎*250-386-3431*).

By Bus

The new intermodal **Pacific Central Station** was opened in 1993 in the old Via Station to allow travellers to connect between bus, train and public transportation in one place. Buses provide several links with the main cities in the province.

Greyhound Lines of Canada
Pacific Central Station
1150 Station St.
☎*482-8747 or 800-661-8747*

Greyhound
☎*482-8747*
also offers service to Nanaimo

Pacific Coach Lines
☎*662-8074*
offers service to Victoria

West Coast Express
☎*683-RAIL*

Vancouver Main Bus Station
☎*683-8133*

Pacific Coach Lines
to Victoria
☎*662-8074*

By Car

Vancouver is accessible by the **Trans-Canada Highway 1** which runs east-west. This national highway links all of the major Canadian cities. It has no tolls and passes through some spectacular scenery. Coming from Alberta, you will pass through the Rocky Mountains, desert regions and a breathtaking canyon.

The city is generally reached from the east by taking the "Downtown" exit from the Trans-Canada. If you are coming from the United States or from Victoria by ferry, you will enter the city on Highway 99 North; in this case expect it to take about 30min to reach downtown.

Driver's licenses from Western European countries are valid in Canada and the United States. While North American travellers won't have any trouble adapting to the rules of the road in Western Canada, European travellers may need a bit more time to get used to things. Here are a few hints:

Rules of the Road

Drivers in western Canada are particularly courteous when it comes to **pedestrians**. They willingly stop to give them the right of way even in big cities, so as a driver keep an eye out for pedestrians. Pedestrian crosswalks are usually indicated by a white sign.

Turning **right on a red light** when the way is clear is permitted in British Columbia.

When a **school bus** (usually yellow in colour) has stopped and has its signals flashing, you must come to a complete stop, no matter what direction you are travelling in. Failing to stop at the flashing signals is considered a serious offense, and carries a heavy penalty.

Wearing of **seatbelts** in the front and back seats is mandatory at all times.

Almost all highways in Western Canada are toll-free, and just a few bridges have tolls. The **speed limit** on highways is 100 km/h. The speed limit on secondary highways is 90 km/h, and 50 km/h in urban areas.

Because Canada produces its own crude oil, **gasoline** (petrol) prices are much less expensive than in Europe, and only slightly more than in the United States. Some gas stations (especially in the downtown areas) might ask for payment in advance as a security measure, especially after 11pm.

Accidents and Emergencies

In case of serious accident, fire or other emergency dial ☎911 or 0. Parts of the interior and Vancouver Island do not have 911.

If you run into trouble on the highway, pull onto the shoulder of the road and turn the hazard lights on. If it is a rental car, contact the rental company as soon as possible. Always file an accident report. If a disagreement arises over who was at fault in an accident, ask for police help.

Finding Your Way Around

By Car

Driving in the City

Getting around Vancouver by car is easy. Take note, however, that the government has decided not to build any expressways through downtown which is exceptional for a city of 1.7 million people; as a result rush-hour traffic can be quite heavy. If you have the time, by all means explore the city on foot.

Practical Information

Car Rentals

Packages including air travel, hotel and car rental (or just hotel and car rental) are often less expensive than car rental alone. It is best to shop around. Remember also that some companies offer corporate rates and discounts to auto-club members. Some travel agencies work with major car rental companies (Avis, Budget, Hertz, etc.) and offer good values; contracts often include added bonuses (reduced ticket prices for shows, etc.).

When renting a car, find out if the contract includes unlimited kilometres, and if the insurance provides full coverage (accident, property damage, hospital costs for you and passengers, theft).

Certain credit cards, gold cards for example, cover the collision and theft insurance. Check with your credit card company before renting.

To rent a car, you must be at least 21 years of age and have had a driver's license for **at least** one year. If you are between 21 and 25, certain companies (for example Avis, Thrifty, Budget) will ask for a $500 deposit, and in some cases they will also charge an extra sum for each day you rent the car. These conditions do not apply for those over 25 years of age.

A credit card is extremely useful for the deposit to avoid tying up large sums of money.

Most rental cars come with an automatic transmission; however you can request a car with a manual shift.

Child safety seats cost extra.

Car Rental Companies

You can rent a car at the airport or in the city.

Tilden
1128 West Georgia St.
☎*685-6111, 800-227-7368 or 800-CAR-RENT*

at the airport
☎*273-3121*

Budget
450 West Georgia St.

at the airport
☎*668-7000 or 800-268-8900* (from Canada)
☎*800-527-0700* (from the U.S.)

ABC Rent-a-Car
255 West Broadway
☎*873-6622 or 800-464-6422*

Thrifty
1400 Robson St.
☎*681-4869*
at the airport
☎*276-0800*

Avis
757 Hornby St.
☎*606-2847*

at the airport
☎*606-2847*

**Exotic Car and
Motorcycle Rentals**
1820 Burrard St.
☎*736-9130 or 644-9128*

Dollar Rent-a-Car
☎*800-800-4000*

Lo-Cost Rent-a-Car
☎*689-9664*

By Taxi

Hailing a taxi in Vancouver is not a problem, especially near the entrances of big downtown hotels and along main arteries such as Robson Street and Georgia Street. The main taxi companies are:

Yellow Cab
☎*681-1111*

McLure's
☎*731-9211*

Black Top
☎*731-1111*
☎*871-1111* (wheelchair accessible taxis)

Vancouver Limousine Service
☎*421-5585 or 888-515-5565*

Public Transportation

BC Transit bus route maps are available from the Vancouver Travel InfoCentre *(summer, every day 8am to 6pm; rest of the year, Mon to Fri 8:30am to 5pm, Sat 9am to 5pm; 200 Burrard St.,* ☎*683-2000)* or from the BC Transit offices in Surrey *(13401 108th Ave., Fifth floor, Surrey, B.C.,* ☎*800-903-4731 or 540-3450)*.

BC Transit also includes a rail transit system and a marine bus. The **Skytrain** runs east from the downtown area to Burnaby, New Westminster and Surrey. These automatic trains run from 5am to 1am all week, except Sundays when they start at 9am. The **Seabus** shuttles frequently between Burrard Inlet and North Vancouver.

Tickets and passes are available for **BC Transit**, including Skytrain and Seabus tickets from the coin-operated machines at some stops, in some convenience stores or by calling ☎261-5100 or 521-0400.

The fares are the same whether you are travelling on a BC Transit bus, the Skytrain or the Seabus. A single ticket generally costs $1.75 for adults and $0.80 for seniors, children and students (must have BC

Transit GoCard), except at peak hours (Mon to Fri before 9:30am and 3pm to 6:30pm) when the system is divided into three zones. It costs $1.75 for travel within one zone, $2.50 within two zones and $3.50 within three zones.

**BC Transit
lost and found
☎682-7887**

**Blue Bus
☎985-7777**
serves West Vancouver

**Car & Van Pooling
☎879-RIDE**

Handicapped Transportation

Handydart
300-3200 East 54th St.
☎430-2692
This company provides public transportation for people who use wheelchairs. You must reserve your seat in advance.

Vancouver Taxis
2205 Main St.
☎255-5111 or 874-5111
They also offers transportation for wheelchair users.

On Foot

The best way to truly appreciate the many facets of any city is generally by foot. This guide outlines nine walking tours in different neighbourhoods. Don't forget your walking shoes!

Drivers in Vancouver are particularly courteous when it comes to **pedestrians**, and willingly stop to give them the right of way even in big cities; so be careful when and where you step off the curb. Pedestrian crosswalks are usually indicated by a white sign. When driving pay special attention that nobody is about to cross near these signs.

By Ferry

The ferry between Granville Island and the Hornby Street dock runs from 7am to 8pm. For information, contact **Granville Island Ferries** (*☎684-7781*) or **Aquabus Ferries** (*☎689-5858*).

Insurance

Cancellation Insurance

Your travel agent will usually offer you cancellation insurance when you buy your airline ticket or vacation package. This insurance allows you to be reimbursed for the ticket or package deal if you must cancel your trip due to serious illness or death. Healthy people are unlikely to need this protection, which is therefore only of relative use.

Theft Insurance

Most residential insurance policies protect some of your goods from theft even if it occurs in a foreign country. To make a claim, you must fill out a police report. It may not be necessary to take out further insurance, depending on the amount covered by your current home policy. As policies vary considerably, you are advised to check with your insurance company. European visitors should take out baggage insurance.

Life Insurance

Several airline companies offer a life insurance plan included in the price of the airplane ticket. However, many travellers already have this type of insurance and do not require additional coverage.

Health Insurance

This is the most useful kind of insurance for travellers, and should be purchased before your departure. Your insurance plan should be as complete as possible because health care costs add up quickly.

When buying insurance, make sure it covers all types of medical costs such as hospitalization, nursing services and doctor's fees. Make sure your limit is high enough, as these expenses can be costly. A repatriation clause is also vital in case the required care is not available on site. Furthermore, since you may have to pay immediately, check your policy to see what provisions it includes for such situations. To avoid any problems during your vacation, always keep proof of your insurance policy on your person.

Health

General Information

Vaccinations are not necessary for people coming from Europe, the United States, Australia and New Zealand. On the other hand, it is strongly suggested, particularly for medium or long-term stays, that visitors take out health and accident insurance. There are different types so it is best to shop around. Bring along all medication, especially prescription medicine. Unless otherwise stated, the water is drinkable throughout British Columbia.

Practical Information

Emergency Phone Numbers

Police: ☎911, Vancouver ☎665-3535, Burnaby ☎294-7922

Firefighters: ☎911, Vancouver ☎665-6000, Burnaby ☎294-7190

Ambulance: ☎872-5151

Crime Stoppers: ☎669-8477

Emergency Hospital: ☎875-4995
To consult a family doctor, contact one of the many clinics, often open from 9am to 10pm, 7 days a week (leaf through the yellow pages or call directory assistance at ☎411).

Dental Emergency: ☎736-3621 (College of Dental Surgeons). There are several dental clinics in the area (consult the yellow pages or call ☎411).

Poison Centre: ☎682-5050 or 682-2344

Crisis Centre (in case of emotional trauma): ☎872-3311

Veterinary Emergency Clinic (24 hours/day): ☎734-5104

Children's Emergency Help Line: dial 0 and ask for "Zenith 1234."

Help for Women: ☎872-8212

Legal Aid: ☎687-4680. 24hr information service on laws in effect in British Columbia.

Roadside Assistance: ☎295-2222 (BCAA)

During the summer, always protect yourself against sunburn. It is often hard to feel your skin getting burned by the sun on windy days. Do not forget to bring sun screen!

Canadians from outside British Columbia should take note that in general your province's health care system will only reimburse you for the cost of any hospital fees or procedures at the going rate in your province. For this reason, it is a good idea to get additional private insurance. In case of accident or illness, make sure to keep your receipts in order to be reimbursed by your province's health care system.

Emergencies

In case of emergency (police, fire department, ambulance), dial ☎911.

Hospitals

Children's Hospital
☎875-2345

Vancouver General Hospital
☎875-4111

Burnaby Hospital
☎434-4211

Lions Gate Hospital
☎988-3131

St. Paul's Hospital
☎682-2344

University Hospital
☎822-7121

Climate and Packing

The climate of Canada varies widely from one region to another. The Vancouver area benefits from a sort of micro-climate thanks to its geographic location between the Pacific Ocean and the mountains. Temperatures in Vancouver vary between 0°C and 15°C in the winter and much warmer in the summer.

If you plan on visiting other regions in Western Canada, keep in mind factors like wind and altitude that can cause a variety of weather conditions. Winters are cold and dry and temperatures can drop to -40°C, though the average is about -20°C. Summers are dry with temperatures staying steady around 25°C in the south and lower in the mountains.

Weather
Environment Canada
☎664-9010

Winter

Vancouver has a particularly wet winter so don't forget your raincoat. In southern British Columbia the mer-

Practical Information

cury rarely falls below 0°C. December to March remains the ideal season for winter-sports enthusiasts who can enjoy many activities not far from the city (skiing, skating, etc.). During this season, it's essential to wear warm clothing (coat, scarf, hat, gloves, wool sweaters and boots) if you plan on visiting the mountains.

Spring and Fall

In Vancouver, spring and fall, and winter too for that matter, are hardly discernable. Spring is short (end of March to end of May), and conditions are generally rainy. Warmer temperatures encourage a beautiful blossoming of flowers. Fall is often cool and wet. A sweater, scarf, gloves, windbreaker and of course an umbrella are recommended for these low seasons.

Summer

Summer lasts from May to the end of August. Bring along T-shirts, lightweight shirts and pants, shorts and sunglasses; a sweater or light jacket is a good idea for evenings. If you plan on doing any hiking, remember that temperatures are cooler at higher altitudes.

Accommodations

A wide choice of types of accommodation to fit every budget is available in Vancouver. Most places are very comfortable and offer a number of extra services. Prices vary according to the type of accommodation and the quality-to-price ratio is generally good. But remember to add the 7% G.S.T (federal Goods and Services Tax) and the provincial sales tax of 7%.

Average Daily High Temperatures °C/°F

Month	Temp	Month	Temp
January	5/41	July	23/74
February	7/44	August	23/74
March	10/50	September	18/65
April	14/58	October	14/58
May	18/65	November	96/48
June	21/69	December	6/43

The Goods and Services Tax is refundable for non-residents in certain cases (see p 57). A credit card will make reserving a room much easier, since payment for the first night is required in most cases.

Many hotels offer corporate discounts as well as discounts for automobile club (CAA, AAA) members. Be sure to ask about these special rates as they are generally very easy to obtain. Furthermore, check in the travel brochures given out at tourist offices since there are often coupons inside.

Hotels

Hotels rooms abound, and range from modest to luxurious. Most hotel rooms come equipped with private bathrooms. There are several internationally reputed hotels in Vancouver.

Inns

Often set up in beautiful historic houses, inns offer quality lodging. There are a lot of these establishments which are more charming and usually more picturesque than hotels. Many are decorated with beautiful period furniture. Breakfast is often included.

Bed and Breakfasts

Unlike hotels or inns, rooms in private homes are not always equipped with private bathrooms. There are many bed and breakfasts in Vancouver. Besides the obvious price advantage, the unique family atmosphere of these establishments is a plus. Credit cards are not always accepted in bed and breakfasts.

The following B&B associations can help you plan a stay in a bed and breakfast by providing addresses and occasionally making your reservations for you:

Beachside Bed & Breakfast Registry
42008 Evergreen Ave.
West Vancouver, V7H 1H1
☎*922-7773*
⇄*926-8073*

Old English Bed & Breakfast Registry
1226 Silverwood Cresc.
North Vancouver, V7P 1J3
☎*986-5069*
⇄*986-8810*

Best Canadian Bed & Breakfast Network
1064 Balfour Ave.
Vancouver, V6H 1X1
☎*738-7207*
⇄*732-4998*

Practical Information

Homestays

Regency International Cultural Exchange & Homestay Inc.
1475 11th Ave. W., apt. 102
V6H 1K9
☎*736-9123*
can arrange homestays for short or long periods for families, business people or students.

Motels

There are many motels on the main access roads into the city. Though they tend to be cheaper, they often lack atmosphere. These are particularly useful when you are pressed for time.

University Residences

Due to certain restrictions, this can be a complicated alternative. Residences are generally only available during the summer (mid-May to mid-August). Reservations must be made several months in advance, usually by paying the first night with a credit card.

This type of accommodation, however, is less costly than the "traditional" alternatives, and making the effort to reserve early can be worthwhile. Visitors with valid student cards can expect to pay approximately $25 plus tax. Bedding is included in the price, and there is usually a cafeteria in the building (meals are not included in the price).

Restaurants

Excellent restaurants are easy to find in Vancouver. As an international crossroads of sorts, you can dine on just about anything in this city. A strong Asian presence and the proximity of the sea have a considerable effect of the types of cuisine offered. You'll also find restaurants in every budget range from fast-food to fine dining.
Prices in this guide are for a meal for one person, excluding drinks and tip.

$	less than $10
$$	$10 to $20
$$$	$20 to $30
$$$$	more than $30

Entertainment

Bars and Nightclubs

In most cases there is no cover charge, aside from the occasional mandatory coat-check. However, expect to pay a few dollars to get into discos on weekends. The legal drinking age is 19; if you're close to that age, expect to be asked for proof.

Wine, Beer and Alcohol

The legal drinking age is 19. Beer, wine and alcohol can only be purchased in liquor stores (closed on Sun) run by the provincial government. Stores specializing in beer and wine are also scattered across the city.

Shopping

In general, prices indicated on price tags for all goods do not include the sales tax (see below).

What to Buy

Salmon: you'll find this fish on sale, fresh from the sea, throughout the coastal areas of British Columbia.

Local crafts: paintings, sculptures, woodworking items, ceramics, copper-based enamels, weaving, etc.

Aboriginal Arts & Crafts: beautiful sculptures made from different types of stone, wood and even animal bone are available, though they are generally quite expensive. Make sure the sculpture is authentic by asking for a certificate of authenticity issued by the Canadian government.

Money and Banking

Currency

The monetary unit is the dollar ($), which is divided into cents (¢). One dollar=100 cents.

Bills come in 5-, 10-, 20-, 50-, 100-, 500- and 1000-dollar denominations, and coins come in 1- (pennies), 5- (nickels), 10- (dimes), 25-cent pieces (quarters), and in 1-dollar (loonies) and 2-dollar (twoonies) coins.

Exchange

Most banks readily exchange American and European currencies but almost every one of these will charge a **commission**. There are, however, exchange offices that do not charge commissions and keep longer hours. Just remember to **ask about fees** and to **compare rates**.

Custom House Currency Exchange
375 Water St.
☎*482-6006*

International Securities Exchange
1169 Robson St.
☎*683-9666*

Practical
Information

Exchange Rates

$1 US	=	$1.47 CAN		$1 CAN	=	$0.68 US
$1 Euro	=	$1.43 CAN		$1 CAN	=	0.70 Euro
£1	=	$2.30 CAN		$1 CAN	=	£0.43
$1 Aust	=	$0.89 CAN		$1 CAN	=	$1.12 Aust
$ NZ	=	$0.71 CAN		$1 CAN	=	$1.41 NZ
1 fl	=	$0.65 CAN		$1 CAN	=	1,54 fl
1 SF	=	$0.88 CAN		$1 CAN	=	1.13 SF
10 BF	=	$0.35 CAN		$1 CAN	=	28.25 BF
1 DM	=	$0.73 CAN		$1 CAN	=	1.37 DM
100 PTA	=	$0.86 CAN		$1 CAN	=	116.52 PTA
1000 ITL	=	$0.74 CAN		$1 CAN	=	1.356 ITL

Thomas Cook
701 Granville
☎687-6111

Money Services
Money Mart
24 hrs/day
☎606-9522 or 606-9612

Traveller's Cheques

Traveller's cheques are accepted in most large stores and hotels. However it is easier and to your advantage to change your cheques at an exchange office. For a better exchange rate, buy your traveller's cheques in Canadian dollars before leaving.

Credit Cards

Most major credit cards are accepted at stores, restaurants and hotels. While the main advantage of credit cards is that they allow visitors to avoid carrying large sums of money, using a credit card also makes leaving a deposit for car rental much easier. Some cards, gold cards for example, automatically insure you when you rent a car (check with your credit card company to see what coverage it provides). In addition, the exchange rate with a credit card is generally better. The most commonly accepted credit cards are Visa, MasterCard, and American Express.

Banks

Banks can be found almost everywhere and most offer the standard services to tourists. Visitors who choose to stay in Canada for a long period of time should note that **non-residents** cannot open bank accounts. If this is the case, the best way to have money readily available is to use traveller's cheques. Withdrawing money from foreign accounts is expensive. However, several automatic teller machines accept foreign bank cards, so that you can withdraw directly from your account. Money orders are another means of having money sent from abroad. No commission is charged but it takes time. People who have resident status, permanent or not (such as landed immigrants, students), can open a bank account. A passport and proof of resident status are required.

Taxes

The ticket price on items usually **does not include tax**. There are two taxes, the GST or federal Goods and Services Tax, of 7% and the PST or Provincial Sales Tax of 7%. They are not cumulative and must be added to the price of most items and to restaurant and hotel bills.

Some hotels charge an additional 8% provincial room tax.

There are some exceptions to this taxation system, such as books, which are only taxed with the GST and food (except for ready made meals), which is not taxed at all.

Tax Refunds for Non-Residents

Non-residents can obtain refunds for the GST paid on purchases. To obtain a refund, it is important to keep your receipts. Refunds up to $500 are obtained instantly from participating duty-free shops when leaving the country or by mailing a special filled-out form to Revenue Canada.

For information, call:
☎ *800-66-VISIT*,
☎ *800-668-4748* in Canada, or
☎ *(902) 432-5608* from outside Canada.

Tipping

In general, tipping applies to all table service: restaurants, bars and night-clubs (therefore no tipping in fast-food restaurants). Tips are also given in taxis and in hair salons.

The tip is usually about 15% of the bill before taxes,

but varies of course depending on the quality of service.

Mail

Canada Post provides efficient (depending on who you talk to) mail service across the country. At press time, it cost $0.46 to send a letter elsewhere in Canada, $0.55 to the United States and $0.95 overseas. Stamps can be purchased at post offices and in many pharmacies and convenience stores.

CANADA POST
General Information
☎800-267-1177
Rates
24 hrs/day
☎662-7222
Postal Codes
☎800-267-1133

Telecommunications

The area code for telephone numbers in this guide is 604 unless otherwise indicated.

The area code for Vancouver and the lower mainland is ☎604. The area code for Vancouver Island, eastern, central and northern British Columbia is ☎250.

Long distance charges are cheaper than in Europe, but more expensive than in the U.S. Pay phones can be found everywhere, often in the entrances of larger department stores and in restaurants. They are easy to use and most accept credit cards. Local calls to the surrounding areas cost $0.25 for unlimited time. Have a lot of quarters on hand if you are making a long distance call. It is less expensive to call from a private residence. 1-800 and 1-888 numbers are toll free.

TELUS sells phone cards in various denominations for use in pay phones to place local and long distance calls.

You can have a phone installed for the length of your stay by calling **TELUS** at ☎888-811-2323.

Holidays

The following is a list of public holidays in the province of British Columbia. Most administrative offices and banks are closed on these days.

New Year's Day: January 1

Easter Monday and/or Good Friday
Victoria Day: third Monday in May

Canada Day: July 1

Civic holiday (British Columbia Day): first Monday in August

Labour Day: first Monday in September

Thanksgiving: second Monday in October

Remembrance Day: November 11 (only banks and federal government services are closed)

Christmas Day: December 25

Boxing Day: December 26

Business Hours

Stores

Stores generally remain open the following hours:

Mon to Fri	10am to 6pm
Thu and Fri	10am to 9pm
Sat	9am or 10am to 5pm
Sun	noon to 5pm

Well-stocked convenience stores are found throughout Vancouver and are open sometimes 24hrs a day.

Banks

Banks are open Monday to Friday from 10am to 4pm. Some are open on Thursdays and Fridays until 6pm or even 8pm and on weekends. Automatic teller machines are widely available and are open night and day.

Post Offices

Large post offices are open Monday to Friday from 9am to 5pm. There are also several smaller post offices located in shopping malls, convenience stores, and even pharmacies; these post offices stay open much later than the larger ones.

Safety

By taking the normal precautions, there is no need to worry about your personal security. If trouble should arise, remember to dial ☎*911*.

Travellers with Disabilities

The BC Coalition of People with Disabilities
204-456 West Broadway
Vancouver, V5Y 1R3
☎*875-0188*
For information on wheelchair accessible attractions, banks, churches, parks, restaurants, stores and theatres get a copy of *Accessibility Awareness Vancouver Guide*.

Public transportation is available from Handy Dart (see p 48).

Practical
Information

Weights and Measures

Weights
1 pound (lb) = 454 grams (g)

Linear Measure
1 kilogram (kg) = 2.2 pounds (lbs)
1 inch = 2.2 centimetres (cm)
1 foot (ft) = 30 centimetres (cm)
1 mile = 1.6 kilometres (km)
1 kilometres (km) = 0.63 miles (mi)
1 metre (m) = 39.37 inches (in)

Land Measure
1 acre = 0.4 hectares (ha)
1 hectare (ha) = 2.471 acres

Volume Measure
1 U.S. gallon (gal) = 3.79 litres
1 U.S. gallon (gal) = 0.83 imperial gallons

Temperature
To convert °F into °C:
subtract 32, divide by 9, multiply by 5

To convert °C into °F:
multiply by 9, divide by 5, add 32

Children

Like in the rest of Canada, facilities exist in Vancouver that make travelling with children easy, whether it be for getting around or when enjoying the sights.

Generally children under five travel for free, and those under 12 are eligible for fare reductions. The same applies for various leisure activities and shows. Find out before you purchase tickets. High chairs and children's menus are available in most restaurants, while a few of the larger stores provide a babysitting service while parents shop.

Daylight Savings Time (+ 1hr) begins the first Sunday in April and ends on the last Sunday in October.

Advice for Smokers

As in the United States, cigarette smoking is considered taboo, and it is being prohibited in more and more public places. A Vancouver by-law prohibits smoking in all public places to which minors have access. This includes all restaurants and food courts in shopping malls, but does not include adult-only establishments which can designate smoking areas. The by-law applies only to the city of Vancouver proper, and therefore has limited scope; nevertheless check before lighting up!

Most public places have smoking and non-smoking sections. Cigarettes are sold in bars, grocery stores, newspaper and magazine shops. As of January 1, 1997, all restaurants in Vancouver are non-smoking.

Time Zone

Vancouver is on Pacific Standard Time. It is 3hrs behind Montreal and New York City, 8hrs behind the United Kingdom and 9hrs behind continental Europe.

Electricity

Voltage is 110 volts throughout Canada, the same as in the United States. Electricity plugs have two parallel, flat pins, and adaptors are available here.

Illegal Drugs

Recreational drugs are illegal and are not tolerated (even "soft" drugs). Anyone caught with drugs in their possession risks severe consequences.

Laundromats

Laundromats are found almost everywhere in urban areas. In most cases detergent is sold on site. Although change machines are sometimes provided, it is best to bring plenty of quarters ($0.25) with you.

Movie Theatres

There are no ushers and therefore no tips. Movie listings can be found in major newspapers. Movie tickets are considerably cheaper on Tuesdays.

Practical Information

Museums

Most museums charge admission. Reduced prices are available for people over 60, for children, and for students. Call the museum for further details.

Newspapers

The two principal newspapers in Vancouver are the *Vancouver Sun* and the *Vancouver Province*.

Pharmacies

In addition to the smaller drug stores, there are large pharmacy chains that sell everything from chocolate to laundry detergent as well as the more traditional items such as cough drops and headache medications.

Shopper's Drug Mart is one of the largest chains of pharmacies in the city. Some of its branches are open 24hrs a day, for addresses see the "Shopping" chapter, p 191.

Another large pharmacy in Vancouver is London Drugs, which can be found throughout the city.

Religion

Almost all religions are represented.

Restrooms

Public restrooms can be found in most shopping centres. If you cannot find one, it usually is not a problem to use one in a bar or restaurant.

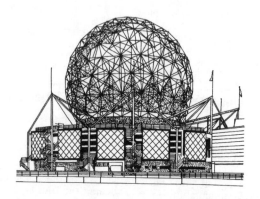

Exploring

The following nine tours, each covering a different part of Vancouver, will help you fully enjoy the local sights.

You can set out to explore the city's streets by taking:

Tour A: Gastown ★

Tour B: Chinatown and East Vancouver ★★

Tour C: Downtown ★★

Tour D: The West End ★

Tour E: Stanley Park ★★★

Tour F: Burrard Inlet ★★★

Tour G: False Creek ★

Tour H: Shaughnessy and South Vancouver ★★

Tour I: The West Side ★★★

Carrall Street serves as the dividing line between east and west in the centre of town (south of False Creek the border between east and west is Ontario Street).

It also marks the border between Gastown to the west, and Chinatown to the east.

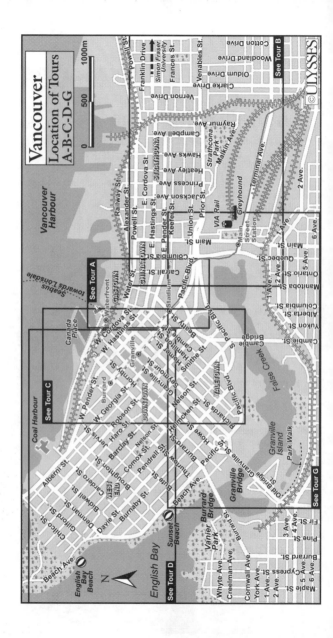

The Vancouver Museum, whose dome resembles the headdress worn by the Coast Salish Indians.
- *Sheila Naiman*

me nightfall, the city is flected in the earby Pacific Ocean.
Tibor Bognàr

The Totem Poles in Stanley Park are reminders of the sizeable Aboriginal population that lived on the peninsula 150 years ago. - *T.*

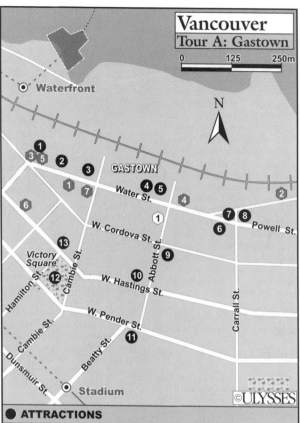

Vancouver
Tour A: Gastown

0   125   250m

Waterfront

N

GASTOWN

Water St.

W. Cordova St.

Powell St.

Victory
Square

Cambie St.

W. Hastings St.

Hamilton St.

Abbott St.

Carrall St.

W. Pender St.

Cambie St.

Beatty St.

Dunsmuir St.

Stadium

©ULYSSES

● ATTRACTIONS

1. Landing Building
2. Hudson House
3. Gastown Steam Clock
4. Gaslight Square
5. Architectural Institute of British Columbia
6. Byrnes Block
7. Maple Tree Square
8. Hotel Europe
9. Lonsdale Block
10. Woodwards
11. Sun Tower
12. Victory Square
13. Dominion Building

⬡ ACCOMMODATIONS

1. The Dominion Hotel

⬡ RESTAURANTS

1. India Village
2. Jewel of India
3. Steamworks Brewing Co.
4. The Old Spaghetti Factory
5. The Raintree
6. Top of Vancouver
7. Water Street Café

Tour A: Gastown

Just a few steps from downtown, Gastown is best discovered on foot. The area dates back to 1867 when John Deighton, known as Gassy Jack, opened a saloon for the employees of a neighbouring sawmill. While Gastown was destroyed by fire in 1886, this catastrophe did not deter the city's pioneers. They rebuilt from the ashes and started anew the development of their city, which was incorporated several months later.

In the late 19th century, Gastown's economic development was driven by rail transport and the gold rush. The neighbourhood then became an important commercial distribution centre, but was later abandoned in favour of areas farther west. After a long period of decline, restoration was begun in the mid-1960s and continues to this day. Gastown's streets are now lined with little hotels, trendy cafés, restaurants, art galleries, souvenir shops and gaslit lanterns. They also make for a pleasant stroll.

Start off your tour at the corner of Water and West Cordova Streets, at the west edge of Gastown, which is accessible from the Waterfront station of the Skytrain.

The **Landing** *(375 Water St.)*, with its brick and stone facade, was a commercial warehouse at the time of its construction in 1905; today it is a fine example of restoration. Since the late 1980s, it has housed offices, shops and restaurants.

Walk east along Water Street.

Like many other 19th-century North American buildings, **Hudson House** *(321 Water St.)* has its back to the water and the natural setting. Erected in 1897 as a warehouse for the Hudson's Bay Company, it was renovated in 1977 in order to accentuate the pure lines of its red brick arches. The **Gastown Steam Clock**, at the corner of Cambie Street, uses steam conducted through an underground network of pipes to whistle the hours. In clear weather, this spot affords a stunning view of the mountains north of the city.

Further along Water Street, you will see the steep roofs of **Gaslight Square** *(131 Water St.)*, a shopping centre laid out around a pretty inner court (Henriquez and Todd, 1975).

Gastown Steam Clock

typical of commercial buildings of the Victorian era. Rising in front is the former **Hotel Europe** *(4 Powell St.)*, a triangular building erected in 1908 by a Canadian hotel-keeper of Italian descent.

Head south on Carrall Street, then turn right onto West Cordova.

Lonsdale Block *(8-28 West Cordova St.)*, built in 1889, is one of the most remarkable buildings on this street. It's undergoing a beautiful renaissance with the recent opening of several shops and, even more importantly, a number of cafés serving all different kinds of coffee made with freshly roasted beans. The coffee trend, which started in the American city of Seattle, less than 200 km from Vancouver, has really taken off along the old-fashioned streets of this neighbourhood. Long popular with artists, Gastown is now considered a tourist area, and unfortunately has become a bit pricey in places.

Nearby are the offices of the **Architectural Institute of British Columbia** ★ *(free; summer Wed to Sun, Sep to May weekends only, 440 Cambie St., Suite 100, schedule and programme, ☎683-8588)*, which offers guided tours of Vancouver during the summertime.

The intersection of Water and Carrall Streets is one of the liveliest parts of Gastown. Long **Byrnes Block** *(2 Water St.)*, on the southwest corner, was one of the first buildings to be erected after the terrible fire of 1886. It was built on the site of Gassy Jack's saloon; a statue of the celebrated barkeep graces tiny **Maple Tree Square**. The thick cornice on the brick building is

Turn left on Abbott Street.

At the corner of Hastings Street stands the former **Woodwards department store** *(101 West Hasting St.)*, founded in 1892 by Charles Woodward. It closed exactly 100 years later, following the death of the Wood-

Exploring

ward family patriarch, and was converted into 350 apartments during the summer of 1996. In the early 20th century, this part of Vancouver was the economic hub of the city. The shift of business to the west had a powerful impact on the area, both socially and economically. Today, part of Gastown is quite poor, and there are many vagrants here. Groups like the Downtown Eastside Residents Association defend the interests of those whose lives have been disrupted by the neighbourhood's recent overhaul. They are attempting to convince authorities to convert abandoned buildings into housing for the needy so that people won't be forced to move to other parts of town.

The south end of Abbott Street is dominated by the **Sun Tower** ★ *(100 West Pender St.)*, erected in 1911 for the *Vancouver World* newspaper. It later housed the offices of the local daily, *The Vancouver Sun*, after which it was named. At the time of its construction, the Sun Tower was the tallest building in all of the British Empire, although it only had 17 floors.

Turn right on West Pender Street to reach Cambie Street and **Victory Square**, in the centre of which stands **The Cenotaph**, a memorial to those who lost their lives in the two World Wars. It was sculpted by Thornton Sharp in 1924. The square acts like a pivot between the streets of Gastown and those of the modern business district. Facing onto the north side is the elegant **Dominion Building** ★ *(207 West Hastings St.)* whose mansard roof is reminiscent of those found on Second Empire buildings along the boulevards of Paris.

Head north on Cambie Street to get back to where you started.

Turn left on West Cordova where you'll find several triangular buildings. They're shaped in accordance with the streets which intersect at different angles. Other buildings, with their series of oriel windows, are reminiscent of San Francisco.

Tour B: Chinatown and East Vancouver

This tour starts at the intersection of Carall and East Pender. On East Pender Street, the scene changes radically. The colour and atmosphere of public markets, plus a strong Chinese presence, bring this street to life. The 1858 Gold Rush in the hinterland drew Chinese from San Francisco and

Vancouver
Tour B: Chinatown and East Vancouver

© ULYSSES

0 250 500m

N

● ATTRACTIONS

1. Sam Kee Building
2. Doctor Sun Yat Sen Garden
3. Lee Building
4. CIBC Building
5. Carnegie Library
6. St. James Anglican Church
7. Little Italy
8. Simon Fraser University

● ACCOMMODATIONS

1. Simon Fraser University

● RESTAURANTS

1. Gain Wah Down
2. Hon's Wun-Tun House
3. Joe's Café
4. Kam Gok Yuen
5. Nick's Spaghetti House
6. Park Lock
7. Santos Tapas Restaurant
8. Sun Sui Wah Seafood Restaurant
9. The Cannery Seafood Restaurant
10. Waa Zuu Bee Café

Hong Kong; in 1878, railway construction brought thousands more Chinese to British Columbia. This community resisted many hard blows that might have ended its presence in the province. At the beginning of the 20th century, the Canadian government imposed a heavy tax on new Chinese immigrants, and then banned Chinese immigration altogether from 1923 to 1947. Today, the local Chinese community is growing rapidly due to the massive influx of immigrants from Hong Kong. Vancouver's Chinatown has now become one of the largest in all of North America.

On your way into Chinatown, you'll see the strange little **Sam Kee Building** *(8 West Pender St.),* which occupies a leftover piece of land barely 2m deep. Its interior space is augmented by the oriel windows overhanging the sidewalk and a basement that extends under the street. This area was once home to several famous brothels as well as to a number of opium dens.

Take East Pender Street into the heart of Chinatown.

It is well worth stopping in at the **Dr. Sun Yat-Sen Garden ★** *(every day 10am to 7:30pm; 578 Carrall St.,* ☎*689-7133)* behind the traditional portal of the **Chinese Cultural Centre** at 50 East Pender St. Built in 1986 by Chinese artists from Suzhou, this garden is the only example outside Asia of landscape architecture from the Ming Dynasty (1368-1644). The 1.2ha green space is surrounded by high walls that create a virtual oasis of peace in the middle of bustling Chinatown. It is worth noting that Dr. Sun Yat-Sen (1866-1925), considered the father of modern China, visited Vancouver in 1911 in order to raise money for his newly founded Kuomintang ("People's Party").

The architecture of the buildings along East Pender Street reflects the background of Vancouver's first Chinese immigrants, most of whom were Cantonese. Take, for example, the deep, multi-storey loggias on a number of the facades, such as that of the **Lee Building ★** *(129 East Pender St.),* built in 1907. To the left of this building is a passageway leading to a charming inner court surrounded by shops.

During Chinese festivals, the loggias along East Pender Street are packed with onlookers, heightening the lively atmosphere.

Turn left on Main Street.

At the corner of East Pender Street stands a branch of the **CIBC (Canadian Imperial Bank of Commerce)** *(501 Main St.)*, whose architecture was inspired by the English baroque style. Faced with terra cotta, this colossal edifice was designed by architect Victor Hosburgh and erected in 1915. Another example of the English baroque revival style is the former **Carnegie Library** *(at the corner of Main and East Hastings)*, now used as a community centre. This building owes its existence to American philanthropist Andrew Carnegie who financed the construction of hundreds of neighbourhood libraries in the United States and Canada.

Turn right on East Cordova Street.

St. James Anglican Church ★ *(303 East Cordova)*, which stands at the corner of Gore Street, is one of the most unusual buildings to be erected in Canada between the two World Wars. A tall, massive structure made of exposed reinforced concrete, it was designed by British architect Adrian Gilbert Scott in 1935.

Head south on Gore Street to admire all the exotic products displayed along East Pender Street or enjoy a meal in one of the many Chinese restaurants there. If you wish to leave no stone unturned in your exploration of Vancouver's ethnic neighbourhoods, take Gore all the way to Keefer, turn right, then take a left on Main Street to reach Pacific Central Station (about a 5min walk). Take the Skytrain toward Surrey, and get off at the next station (Broadway). If you're driving, head east on Georgia Street, turn onto Prior Street at the viaduct, then take a right on Commercial Drive.

When you get off the Skytrain, head north up Commercial Drive.

The next part of town you'll pass through is known as **Little Italy**, but is also home to Vancouverites of Portuguese, Spanish, Jamaican and South American descent. In the early 20th century, the Commercial Drive area became the city's first suburb with middle-class residents building small, single-family homes with wooden siding here. The first Chinese and Slavic immigrants moved into the neighbourhood during World War I, and another wave of immigrants, chiefly Italian, arrived at the end of World War II. North Americans will feel pleasantly out

Exploring

of their element in the congenial atmosphere of Little Italy's Italian cafés and restaurants. A few of these are listed in the "Restaurants" chapter (see p 153).

Some of Vancouver's most spectacular attractions are located outside the downtown area. To conclude your tour of East Vancouver, head to the city of Burnaby to visit **Simon Fraser University ★★** (SFU), located about 30min from the centre of Vancouver. If you don't have a car, take Bus #135 to the campus. Otherwise, drive east on East Hastings Street, take a right on Sperling Avenue, then a left on Curtis Street, which turns into Gagliardi Way.

Perched atop Burnaby Mountain, SFU looks like a huge spaceship that just arrived here from another galaxy. The campus offers a panoramic view of downtown Vancouver, Burrard Inlet and the towering mountains to the north – a breathtaking sight in clear weather. The main buildings of bare concrete that form the nucleus of the university were designed in 1963 by western Canada's star architect Arthur Erickson and his associate Geoffrey Massey. Their architecture reflects the influence of Japanese temples, European cloisters, Mayan ruins and the Californian

practice of leaving large parts of the exterior open. The grouping is laid out around a large courtyard. There is also a mall, half of which is sheltered by a glass and metal structure so that students can enjoy pleasant temperatures winter and summer alike and find shelter from the region's frequent rainfalls.

Tour C: Downtown

On May 23, 1887, Canadian Pacific's first transcontinental train, which set out from Montréal, arrived at the Vancouver terminus. The railway company, which had been granted an area roughly corresponding to present-day downtown Vancouver, began to develop its property. To say that it played a major role in the development of the city's business district would be an understatement. Canadian Pacific truly built this part of town, laying the streets and erecting many very important buildings. Downtown Vancouver has been developing continually since the 1960s. It's a sign of the city's great economic vitality, which can be attributed to Asian capital and the English Canadian population's shift westward to the mild climes of the Pacific coast.

This tour starts at the corner of West Hastings and Richards. Head west on West Hastings, toward the Marine Building, which will be directly in your line of vision. This tour can easily be combined with Tour A which covers Gastown and ends nearby.

Located opposite Harbour Centre, the former regional headquarters of the **Toronto Dominion Bank** *(580 West Hastings St.)* exemplify the classical elegance of early 20th-century financial banking halls. The building has since been abandoned by the bank for one of the modern skyscrapers along Georgia Street. The former regional headquarters of the **Canadian Imperial Bank of Commerce** *(640 West Hastings St.)*, a veritable temple of finance, met the same fate and now houses shops. With its massive Ionic columns, this building was erected in 1906 according to a design by Darling and Pearson, whose credits include the Sun Life Building in Montreal. Opposite stands the massive **Royal Bank ★** *(675 West Hastings St.)* building, designed by S. G. Davenport. The Italian Renaissance style banking hall is worth a look.

The **Sinclair Centre ★** *(701 West Hastings St.)* is a group of government offices. It occupies a former post office, and its annexes are connected to one another

by covered passageways lined with shops. The main building, dating from 1909, is considered to be one of the finest examples of the neo-baroque style in Canada.

Sinclair Centre

A little further, at the corner of Hornby Street, is an austere edifice built in 1913 by the **Crédit Foncier Franco-Canadien** *(850 West Hastings St.)*, a financial institution jointly founded by French and Quebecois bankers. On the other side of the street, the **Vancouver Club** *(915 West Hasting St.)* is dwarfed by the skyscrapers on either side of it.

Exploring

● ATTRACTIONS

1. Toronto Dominion Bank
2. CIBC Building
3. Royal Bank
4. Sinclair Centre
5. Crédit Foncier Franco-canadien
6. Vancouver Club
7. Marine Building (R)
8. Canada Place
9. Bentall Centre
10. Royal Centre
11. Vancouver Hotel
12. Christ Church Cathedral
13. Cathedral Place
14. Canadian Craft Museum
15. Robson Street
16. B.C. Hydro Building
17. St. Andrew's Wesley United Church
18. First Baptist Church
19. Provincial Law Courts
20. Robson Square
21. Vancouver Art Gallery
22. Granville Street Mall
23. Pacific Centre
24. The Bay
25. Vancouver Centre
26. Eaton
27. Commodore Theatre
28. Orpheum Theatre
29. Vogue Theatre
30. Yaletown
31. Vancouver Public Library
32. Ford Centre for the Performing Arts
33. Canadian Broadcasting Corporation
34. General Post Office
35. Queen Elizabeth Theatre
36. Cathedral of Our Lady of the Rosary

◌ ACCOMMODATIONS

1. Best Western Downtown Vancouver
2. Bosman's Motor Hotel
3. Canadian Pacific Waterfront Centre Hotel
4. Hampton Inn & Suites
5. Metropolitan Hotel
6. Pan Pacific Vancouver Hotel
7. Sandman Hotel
8. Terminal City Club
9. Travelodge Vancouver Centre
10. Vancouver Hotel (R)
11. Wedgewood Hotel (R)
11. YWCA

(R) establishment with restaurant (see description)

● RESTAURANTS

1. Aqua Riva
2. Arena Ristorante
3. Capone's
4. Dining Car
5. Diva at the Met
6. Dix Barbecue and Brewery
7. DV8
8. Furusato
9. Hard Rock Café
10. India Gate
11. Joe Fortes
12. Kitto
13. Le Crocodile
14. Malone's Bar & Grill
15. Maverick's
16. Planet Hollywood
17. Rodney's Oyster House
18. Settebello
19. Tsunami Sushi
20. White Spot
21. Yaletown Brewing Co.

Founded in 1914, it is a private club for business-men modelled after similar clubs in London.

The **Marine Building** ★★ *(355 Burrard St.)*, which faces straight down West Hastings Street, is a fine example of the Art Deco style. It's characterized by vertical lines, staggered recesses, geometric orna-mentation and the absence

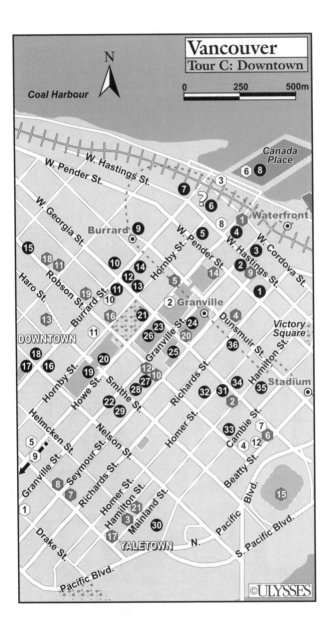

Coal Harbour

N

0   250   500m

Canada Place

W. Hastings St.

W. Pender St.

W. Georgia St.

Burrard

W. Hornby St.

W. Pender St.

Waterfront

W. Hastings St.

W. Cordova St.

Robson St.

Haro St.

Burrard St.

Granville St.

Granville

Dunsmuir St.

Victory Square

DOWNTOWN

Hamilton St.

Stadium

Hornby St.

Howe St.

Smithe St.

Richards St.

Helmcken St.

Nelson St.

Homer St.

Cambie St.

Granville St.

Seymour St.

Richards St.

Beatty St.

Homer St.

Hamilton St.

Pacific Blvd.

Drake St.

Mainland St.

YALETOWN

N.

S. Pacific Blvd.

Pacific Blvd.

©ULYSSES

of a cornice at the top of the structure. Erected in 1929, the building lives up to its name in part because it is lavishly decorated with nautical motifs, and also because its occupants are ship-owners and shipping companies. Its facade features terra cotta panels depicting the history of shipping and the discovery of the Pacific coast. The interior decor is even more inventive, however. The lights in the lobby are shaped like the prows of ships, and there is a stained glass window showing the sun setting over the ocean. The elevators will take you up to the mezzanine which offers an interesting general view of the building.

Take Burrard Street toward the water to reach **Canada Place** ★ ★ (999 Canada Place), which occupies one of the piers along the harbour and looks like a giant sailboat ready to set out across the waves.

This multi-purpose complex, which served as the Canadian pavilion at Expo '86, is home to the city's Convention Centre, the harbour station where ocean liners dock, the luxurious Pan Pacific Hotel (see p 140) and an Imax theatre. Take a walk on the "deck" and drink in the magnificent panoramic view of Burrard Inlet, the port and the snow-capped mountains.

Take Burrard Street back into the centre of town and continue southward to West Georgia Street.

On your way, you'll see the giant **Benttal Centre** *(at the corner of Pender St.)*, made up of three towers designed by architect Frank Masson and erected between 1965 and 1975.

Canada Place

You'll also see the **Royal Centre** *(1055 West Georgia St.)*, which includes the 38-storey Royal Bank tower. These skyscrapers have to be "low" and squat in order to withstand the seismic activity in the Pacific Ring of Fire.

The imposing **Hotel Vancouver ★** *(900 West Georgia St.)* (see p 140), a veritable monument to the Canadian railway companies that built it between 1928 and 1939, stands at the corner of West Georgia Street. For many years, its high copper roof served as the principal symbol of Vancouver abroad. Like all major Canadian cities, Vancouver had to have a Château-style hotel. Make sure to take a look at the gargoyles near the top and the bas-reliefs at the entrance, which depict an ocean liner and a moving locomotive.

The 23-storey hotel dwarfs the tiny **Christ Church Cathedral** *(690 Burrard St.)* facing it. This Gothic Revival Anglican cathedral was built in 1889, back when Vancouver was no more than a large village. Its skeleton, made of Douglas fir, is visible from inside. What is most interesting about the cathedral, however, is neither its size nor its ornamentation, but simply the fact that it has survived in this part of town which is continually being rebuilt.

Flanking the cathedral to the east are the shops and offices of **Cathedral Place** *(925 West Georgia St.)*, built in 1991. Its pseudo-medieval gargoyles have not managed to make people forget about the Art Deco-style Georgia Medical Building, which once occupied this site, and whose demolition in 1989 prompted a nation-wide outcry. Even with rock singer Bryan Adams' help, a major campaign to save the building proved futile. Cathedral Place is thus a building that is trying to gain acceptance. Its pointed roof was modelled after that of the neighbouring hotel, and is adorned with the stone nurses that once graced the Georgia Medical Building. The **Canadian Craft Museum** *($5; Mon to Sat 10am to 5pm, Sun and holidays noon to 5pm, Thu to 9pm, Sep to May closed Tue; 639 Hornby St., ☎687-8266)* lies behind in a pretty little garden integrated into the project. This small, recently built spot houses a sampling of Canadian handicrafts and a few decorative elements that were part of the Georgia Medical Building.

Head west on West Georgia Street.

Turn left on Thurlow Street and left again on **Robson Street ★**, which is lined with fashionable boutiques, elaborately decorated res-

Exploring

taurants and West Coast-style cafés. People sit at tables outside, enjoying the fine weather and watching the motley crowds stroll by. This activity has become a veritable mania among coffee lovers. An American celebrity passing through Vancouver marvelled at the number of cafés on Robson Street, going so far as to declare that Vancouverites are addicted to coffee. If this is true, it hasn't changed the tempo of life here which is known to be quite laid back. In the mid-20th century, a small German community settled around Robson Street, dubbing it Robsonstrasse, a nickname it bears to this day.

Return to Burrard Street, turn right and continue to Nelson Street.

The former **B.C. Hydro Building ★** *(970 Burrard St.)*, at the corner of Nelson and Burrard, was once the head office of the province's hydroelectric company. In 1993, it was converted into a 242-unit co-op and renamed The Electra. Designed in 1955 by local architects Thompson, Berwick and Pratt, it is considered to be one of the most sophisticated skyscrapers of that era in all of North America. The ground floor is adorned with a mural and a mosaic in shades of grey, blue and green, executed

by artist B.C. Binning. On the other side of the street stands **St. Andrew's Wesley United Church** that was built in 1931 and houses a window created by master glassworker Gabriel Loire of Chartres, France in 1969. The **First Baptist Church** *(969 Burrard St.)*, located opposite, was erected in 1911.

Walk east on Nelson Street.

Turn left on Howe Street to view the **Provincial Law Courts ★** *(800 Smithe St.)* (1978), designed by talented Vancouver architect Arthur Erickson. The vast interior space, accented in glass and steal, is worth a visit. The courthouse and **Robson Square** *(on the 800 block of Robson St.)*, by the same architect, form a lovely ensemble. Vancouver's luxuriant vegetation (sustained by abundant rainfall), unlike anything else in Canada, is put to maximum use here. Plants are draped along rough concrete walls and in between multiple little stepped ponds over which little waterfalls flow. Shops, restaurants and a skating rink welcome passers-by.

The **Vancouver Art Gallery ★** *($10; May 3 to Oct 9, Mon to Wed 10am to 6pm, Thu 10am to 9pm, Fri 10am to 6pm, Sat 10am to 5pm, Sun and holidays noon to 5pm, closed Mon and Tue during winter; 750*

Hornby St., ☎*662-4700),* located north of Robson Square, occupies the former Provincial Law Courts. This big, neoclassical-style building was erected in 1908 according to a design by British architect Francis Mawson Rattenbury. His other credits include the British Columbia Legislative Assembly and the Empress Hotel, both located in Victoria on Vancouver Island. Later, Rattenbury returned to his native country and was assassinated by his wife's lover. The museum's collection includes a number of paintings by Emily Carr (1871-1945), a major Canadian painter whose primary subjects were the Aboriginal peoples and landscapes of the West Coast.

Continue along Howe Street.

Turn right on West Georgia Street, then right again on the **Granville Street Mall** ★, the street of cinemas, theatres, nightclubs and retail stores. Its busy sidewalks are hopping 24hrs a day. The black skyscrapers at the corner of West Georgia belong to the **Pacific Centre** *(on either side of Georgia St.),* designed by architects Cesar Pelli and Victor Gruen (1969). A stainless steel sculpture by Greg Norris adorns the public square. Beneath the towers lie the beginnings of an underground city modelled after

Montreal's, with 130 shops and restaurants. Opposite stands the Hudson's Bay Company department store (1913), better known as **The Bay**. The company was founded in London in 1670 in order to carry out fur-trading operations in North America. In 1827, it became one of the first enterprises to set up shop in British Columbia. Across the street stands the **Vancouver Centre** *(650 West Georgia St.),* which contains Scotia Bank's regional headquarters, and the **Vancouver Block** *(736 Granville St.),* topped by an elegant clock. Finally, you can't miss the now-closed, massive white **Eaton** department store south of the Pacific Centre.

Stroll along the Granville Street Mall heading south towards Theatre Row. You'll pass the **Commodore Theatre** *(870 Granville St.)* and the **Orpheum Theatre** ★ *(649 Cambie St., free tour upon reservation* ☎*665-3050).* Behind the latter's narrow facade, barely 8m wide, a long corridor opens onto a 2,800-seat Spanish-style Renaissance Revival theatre. Designed by Marcus Priteca, it was the largest and most luxurious movie theatre in Canada when it opened in 1927. After being meticulously restored in 1977, the Orpheum became the concert hall of the Vancouver Symphony Orchestra. Further south, you'll see the vertical sign of the **Vogue Theatre** *(918 Granville St.)*, erected in 1941. Today, popular musicals are presented in its Streamlined Art Deco hall.

Turn left on Nelson and left again on Homer.

Located in the southeast of the downtown area, **Yaletown** was an industrial area when the railways were still king. The growth of the trucking industry shifted business away from Yaletown's big warehouses with the loading docks of Hamilton and Mainland streets now transformed into outdoor cafés and restaurants. A new group of tenants now occupies the old brick warehouses; designers, architects, film production companies and business people in general have brought this area back to life. Trendy cafés and restaurants have followed suit.

At the corner of Robson Street is a curious building that is somewhat reminiscent of Rome's Coliseum – the **Vancouver Public Library** ★★ *(free admission; year-round, Mon and Tue 10am to 9pm, Wed to Sat 10am to 6pm; Oct to Apr, Sun 1pm to 5pm, closed Sun in the summer; free tours can be arranged, ☎331-4041; 350 West*

Georgia St., ☎*331-3600).* This brand-new building is the work of Montréal architect Moshe Safdie, known for his Habitat '67 in Montréal and the National Art Gallery in Ottawa. The project stirred lively reactions both from local people and from architecture critics. The design was chosen after finally being put to a referendum. The six-storey atrium is positively grandiose. The **Ford Centre for the Performing Arts**, completed in 1996, lies just opposite on Homer Street. Among other things, it contains an 1,800-seat theatre whose orchestra seats, balcony and stage are depicted on the facade north of the glass cone that serves as the entryway. Unfortunately, the Ford Centre is now closed and the City has yet to decide its future.

Vancouver Public Library

Behind the library lies the long, low building of the **Canadian Broadcasting Corporation**. The tubular structures on the facade are actually air ducts. The **General Post Office** *(349 West Georgia St.)*, north of the library, was built in 1953. Hidden behind it to the east is the **Queen Elizabeth Theatre** *(630 Hamilton St.)*, designed chiefly by Montreal architects Ray Affleck and Fred Lebensold. It contains three theatres of different sizes. Its opening in 1959 foreshadowed the construction of similar complexes across North America, including New York's celebrated Lincoln Centre and Montreal's Place des Arts.

Take Homer Street north, then turn right on Dunsmuir Street.

To conclude your tour of downtown Vancouver, stop by the city's Catholic cathedral, the **Cathedral of Our Lady of the Rosary** *(at the corner of Dunsmuir and Richards)*, erected in 1899. The rusticated stone facing and the wood and metal clock towers are reminiscent of parish churches built around the same time in Quebec.

Tour D: The West End

Excluding Vancouver Island, further west, the West End is the end of the line, the final destination of that quest for a better life that thousands of city-dwellers from eastern Canada have been embarking upon for generations. People come here for the climate and the vegetation, no doubt, but also to escape the hustle and bustle and constraints of the older cities in the central and eastern parts of the country. Despite all its concrete skyscrapers, the West End has a laid-back atmosphere that's influenced both by the immensity of the Pacific and the wisdom of the Orient.

As a result of this westward movement, and the fact that there is nowhere to go beyond here, the West End has the highest population per square kilometre of any area in Canada. Fortunately, nature is never far off, what with nearby Stanley Park (see p 86), stunning views of snow-capped mountains from the streets running north-south, or simply the sight of a cackling Canada goose strolling around a busy intersection.

Exploring

● ATTRACTIONS

1. Rogers House
2. Alexandra Park
3. English Bay Beach
4. Ocean Towers
5. Sylvia Hotel
6. Denman Place
7. Coal Harbour
8. Robson Public Market

◐ ACCOMMODATIONS

1. Barclay Hotel
2. Blue Horizon Hotel
3. Buchan Hotel
4. Carmana Plaza
5. Coast Plaza at Stanley Park
6. Greenbrier Apartment Motor Hotel
7. Landmark Hotel (R)
8. Listel O'Doul's Hotel
9. Oceanside Hotel
10. Pacific Palisades Hotel
11. Parkhill Hotel
12. Riviera Motor Inn
13. Robsonstrasse City Motor Inn
14. Rosellen Suites
15. Sheraton Wall Centre Hotel
16. Sylvia Hotel
17. The Burrard Motor Inn
18. The Sutton Place Hotel
19. Tropicana Motor Inn
20. Vancouver's Suites By the Sea
21. West End Guest House Bed & Breakfast
22. Westin Bayshore

(R) establishment with restaurant (see description)

◑ RESTAURANTS

1. Ballantine's Restaurant
2. Bread Garden
3. Chartwell
4. Ciao Espresso Bar
5. Cloud 9 Revolving Restaurant
6. Da Pasta Bar
7. Flying Wedge Pizza Co.
8. Fresgo Inn Restaurant & Bakery
9. Goodfellas
10. Gyoza King
11. L'Hermitage
12. La Crêpe Bretonne
13. Le Café de Paris
14. Le Gavroche
15. Liliget
16. Marbella
17. Mescallero
18. Miko Sushi
19. Milestone's
20. Moose's
21. Raincity Grill
23. Raku
24. Rex Rotisserie & Grill
25. Sakae Japanese Restaurant
26. Starbucks
27. TGI Friday's
28. The Old Bailiff
29. True Confections

This tour starts at the corner of Thurlow and Davie. Head west on the latter.

The population of the West End is a mixture of students and professionals, many of whom are getting rich thanks to new technologies and the various new therapies now in fashion. The gay community is also well represented here. Residents of the local high-rises

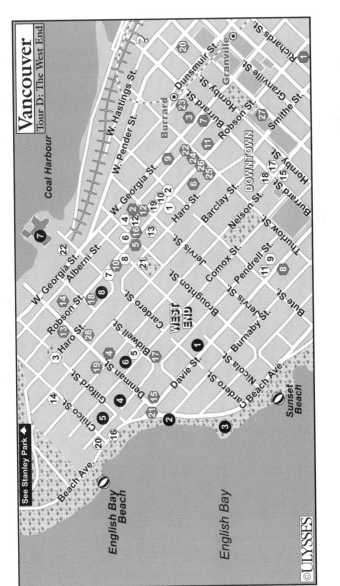

patronize the cafés, fast-food restaurants and grocery stores on **Davie Street** *(between Thurlow and Jervis)*. When you get to the corner of Nicola Street, take a look at **Rogers House** *(1531 Davie St.)*, christened Gabriola by its owner when it was built in 1900. It was designed by one of the most prolific architects of well-heeled Vancouver society, Samuel Maclure. The house, with its numerous chimneys and circular gazebo, originally belonged to sugar magnate Benjamin Tingley Rogers, a native of New York. At the turn of the 20th century, the West End seemed destined to become an affluent suburb with large houses surrounded by gardens. One street was even given the pretentious name Blue Blood Alley. Things turned out otherwise, however, when the streetcar tracks were laid and a popular public beach on English Bay was opened in 1912. Gabriola is one of the only remaining houses of that era, and has since been converted into a restaurant.

Head west on Davie Street, then left on Bidwell Street to reach **Alexandra Park** ★ which forms a point south of Burnaby Street. It boasts a pretty wooden bandstand (1914) for outdoor concerts, as well as a marble fountain adorned with a brass plaque honouring Joe Fortes, who taught several generations of the city's children to swim. This luxuriant park also offers a splendid view of **English Bay Beach** ★★ *(along the shore between Chilco and Bidwell Sts.)*, whose fine sands are crowded during the summer. The apartment high-rises behind it give beach-goers the illusion that they are lounging about at a seaside resort like Acapulco, when they are actually just a short distance from the heart of Vancouver. Few cities can boast beaches so close to their downtown core. Fleets of sailboats skim across the magnificent bay which has recently been cleaned of pollutants. To the west, it is bordered by the verdant expanse of Stanley Park (see p 86).

After dipping your big toe in the Pacific Ocean (it's that close!), head back into town on Morton Avenue where you'll see the **Ocean Towers** *(1835 Morton Ave.)*, a cluster of jazzily shaped apartment buildings dating from 1957 (Rix Reinecke, architect). The previous year, Vancouver had modified the zoning regulation for the West End so that these high-rises could be built. That provoked a frenzy among real-estate developers and led to the construction of an interesting group of buildings that is as 1950s and "piña colada" as Miami Art Deco is

1930s and "dry martini". The Ocean Towers' neighbour to the west, the **Sylvia Hotel** (p 142) *(1154 Gilford St.)* is the oldest building on the beach. Its construction in 1912 sounded the death knell of the West End's country atmosphere. It is flanked by two post-modern buildings, **Eugenia Tower** and **Sylvia Tower**, topped in a very amusing fashion.

Head back east to Denman Street.

When they're not out surfing or sailboarding, the local beach bums often hang out around Denman and Davie Streets. The numerous restaurants in this area serve gargantuan brunches.

Continue north on Denman Street.

Denman Place *(1733 Comox St.)*, at the corner of Comox Street, is a multi-functional complex made of bare concrete. Erected in 1968, it is home to the West End's largest shopping mall, complete with a supermarket, stores and movie theatres. The commercial area is topped by a 32-storey tower containing apartments and a hotel.

Continue to the north end of Denman Street.

Take the path beside 1779 West Georgia Street to the waterfront and lovely **Coal Harbour ★**, which offers some outstanding views of Stanley Park and the mountains. You will also be greeted by a rather strange sight along the docks: a floating village of houseboats. The bay is full of yachts and sailboats, adding to the West End's seaside charm.

Go back to West Georgia, then take Bidwell south to Robson.

Head east on Robson Street, to the **Robson Public Market ★** *(1610 Robson, at the corner of Cardero)*, a bustling indoor market with a long glass roof. You'll find everything here from live crabs and fresh pasta to local handicrafts. You can also eat here, as dishes from all over the world are served on the top floor. A pleasure for both the palate and the eyes!

If your legs aren't too tired, take Robson Street east back to downtown Vancouver and Thurlow Street. On the way, you'll pass countless shops, some with very creative window displays. You can also head downtown on bus #19, which runs along Georgia Street (two blocks north). During the ride, you will be treated to some spectacular views of the mountains of North and West Vancouver.

★★★

Tour E: Stanley Park

Lord Stanley, the same person for whom ice hockey's Stanley Cup was named, founded Stanley Park on a romantic impulse back in the 19th century when he was Canada's Governor General (1888-1893). Stanley Park lies on an elevated peninsula stretching into the Georgia Strait, and encompasses 405ha of flowering gardens, dense woodlands and lookouts offering views of the sea and the mountains. Obviously Vancouver's many skyscrapers have not prevented the city from maintaining close ties with the nearby wilderness. Some species are held in captivity, but many others roam free – sometimes even venturing into the West End.

Totem

A 10km waterfront promenade known as the **Seawall** runs around the park, enabling pedestrians to drink in every bit of the stunning scenery here. The **Stanley Park Scenic Drive** is the equivalent of the Seawall for motorists. The best way to explore Stanley Park, however, is by bicycle. You can rent one from **Spokes Bicycle Rental** *(corner of West Georgia and Denman,* ☎*688-5141)* (see p 119).

Another way to discover some of the park's hidden treasures is to walk along one of the many footpaths crisscrossing the territory. There are numerous rest areas along the way.

From West Georgia Street, walk along Coal Harbour toward Brockton Point.

You'll be greeted by the sight of scores of gleaming yachts in the Vancouver marina with the downtown skyline in the background. This is the most developed portion of the park, where you'll find the **Malkin Bowl**, the **Brockton Oval** and most importantly, the **Totem Poles** ★ which are reminders of a sizeable Aboriginal population on the peninsula barely 150 years ago.

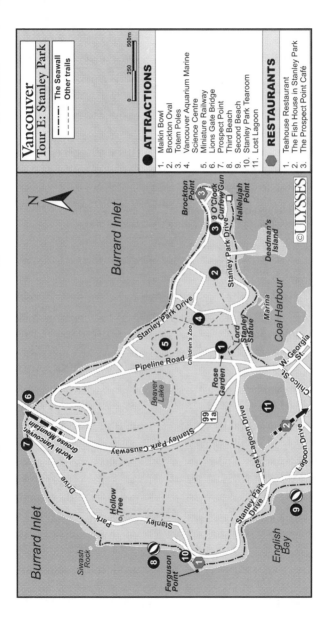

Vancouver
Tour E: Stanley Park

- - - - The Seawall
- - - - Other trails

0   250   500m

● ATTRACTIONS

1. Malkin Bowl
2. Brockton Oval
3. Totem Poles
4. Vancouver Aquarium Marine Science Centre
5. Miniature Railway
6. Lions Gate Bridge
7. Prospect Point
8. Third Beach
9. Second Beach
10. Stanley Park Tearoom
11. Lost Lagoon

⬡ RESTAURANTS

1. Teahouse Restaurant
2. The Fish House in Stanley Park
3. The Prospect Point Café

© ULYSSES

N

Burrard Inlet

Brockton
Point

9 O'Clock
Curfew Gun

Hallelujah
Point

Deadman's
Island

Stanley Park Drive

Marina

Coal Harbour

Stanley Park Drive

Children's Zoo

Rose
Garden

Lord
Stanley
Statue

Pipeline Road

Beaver
Lake

99
1a

Stanley Park Causeway

North Vancouver
■ Grouse Mountain

Park

Drive

Stanley

Hollow
Tree

Siwash
Rock

Burrard Inlet

Ferguson
Point

W. Georgia St.

Chilco St.

Lost Lagoon Drive

Stanley Park Drive

Lagoon Drive

English
Bay

The **9 O'Clock Gun** goes off every day at 9pm on Brockton Point (it is best not to be too close when it does). This shot used to alert fishermen that it was time to come in.

Continue walking along Burrard Inlet.

On the left is the entrance to the renowned **Vancouver Aquarium Marine Science Centre** ★★★ *($13; Jul and Aug, every day 9:30am to 7pm; Sep to Jun, every day 10am to 5:30pm; ☎659-3474)*, which has the undeniable advantage of being located near the ocean.

Dolphin

It displays representatives of the marine animal life of the West Coast and the Pacific as a whole, including magnificent killer whales, belugas, dolphins, seals and exotic fish. The nearby **Miniature Railway** is a real hit with kids.

Stanley Park harbours some lovely **flower gardens** ★ that are meticulously tended by a team of gardeners. Ask for Monsieur Gérard, a French gardener who has been working here for years; he'll show you "his" Stanley Park. Head back to the

Seawall under **Lions Gate Bridge** ★★, an elegant suspension bridge built in 1938. It spans the First Narrows, linking the affluent suburb of West Vancouver to the centre of town. **Prospect Point** ★★★, to the west, offers a general view of the bridge whose steel pillars stand 135m high.

The **Seawall Promenade** runs along the edge the park, and after rounding a 45-degree bend offers a panoramic view of the Georgia Strait, with Cypress Park and Bowen Island visible in the distance on clear days. Next, it passes **Third Beach** ★, one of the most pleasant beaches in the region.

The numerous cargo ships and ocean liners waiting to enter the port complement the setting.

We recommend stopping at the **Stanley Park Tearoom** ★ (see Teahouse Restaurant, p 163), located between Third Beach and **Second Beach** ★. In the 1850s, the British government, fearing an American invasion (the U.S. border is less than 30km from Vancouver), considered building artillery batteries on this site. The risk of such a conflict had diminished by the early 20th century, so a charming tearoom was erected here instead. The Swiss-chalet-style building, surrounded by greenery, dates from 1911.

Complete the loop by taking the path to the **Lost Lagoon** ★, which was once part of Coal Harbour but was partially filled in during the construction of Lions Gate Bridge. It is now a bird sanctuary where large numbers of barnacle geese, mallards and swans can be seen frolicking about.

Tour F: Burrard Inlet

Burrard Inlet is the long and very wide arm of the sea on which the Vancouver harbour – Canada's most important port for over 20 years now – is located. The Atlantic was once a favourite trading route, but the dramatic economic growth of the American West Coast (California, Oregon, Washington) and even more importantly, the Far East (Japan, Hong Kong, Taiwan, China, Singapore, Thailand, etc.), has crowned the Pacific lord and master of shipping.

Beyond the port lie the mountainside suburbs of North and West Vancouver

which offer some spectacular views of the city below. Along their steep, winding roads, visitors can admire some of the finest examples of modern residential architecture in North America. These luxurious houses, often constructed of posts and beams made of local wood, are usually surrounded by lofty British Columbian firs and a luxuriant blend of plants imported from Europe and Asia.

There are two ways to take this tour. The first is by foot: hop aboard the Seabus, the ferry that shuttles back and forth between downtown Vancouver and the north shore of Burrard Inlet, enjoy the open air and take in some exceptional views of both the city and the mountains. The other option is to drive across Lions Gate Bridge (see p 88), take Marine Drive east to Third Street and head south on Lonsdale Avenue. The following descriptions refer to the walking tour, unless otherwise indicated.

Start off your tour in front of the Neo-Classical Revival facade of the former **Canadian Pacific station** ★ *(601 West Cordova St.)*, which dates from 1912 and was designed by Montréal architects Barrott, Blackader and Webster.

Exploring

This station, Canadian Pacific's third in Vancouver, occupies a special place in the city's history. Before ships arriving from the west took over, trains arriving from the east fuelled the area's prosperous economy. In keeping with the times, the station no longer welcomes trains, but provides access to the Granville terminal of the Seabus. It also provides indirect access to the Waterfront terminal of the Skytrain (at the far end of Howe Street), but that's somewhat of a meagre consolation prize. Above the latter terminal is tiny **Portal Park** and its azaleas.

Granville Square, the skyscraper immediately to the west, is the only completed portion of a major real-estate development project (1971) which was to include the demolition of the train station.

Follow the signs for the Seabus. The crossing *($1.75)* takes barely 15min, though you'll wish it were longer. The ferry lands at its northern terminal near the pleasant **Lonsdale Quay Market** ★★, built on a quay stretching out into Burrard Inlet. The cafés surrounding the market offer an unimpeded view of Vancouver

---

● ATTRACTIONS

1. Canadian Pacific Station
2. Granville Square
3. Lonsdale Quay Market
4. Mission Indian Reserve
5. St. Paul Catholic Church
6. Capilano Suspension Bridge and Park
7. Capilano Salmon Hatchery
8. Cleveland Dam Park
9. Grouse Mountain
10. Mount Seymour Provincial Park
11. Deep Cove
12. Baden Powell Trail
13. Ambleside Park
14. Pratt House
15. Berwick House
16. British Properties
17. Lighthouse Park
18. Gordon Smith House
19. Cypress Provincial Park

◯ ACCOMMODATIONS

1. Canyon Court Motel
2. Capilano Bed & Breakfast
3. Globetrotter's Inn
4. Grouse Inn
5. Horseshoe Bay Motel
6. Lonsdale Quay Hotel
7. Palms Guest House
8. Summit View

● RESTAURANTS

1. Beach Side Café
2. Bean Around The World
3. Bino's
4. Bread Garden
5. Bridge House Restaurant
6. Salmon House on the Hill
7. The Boathouse

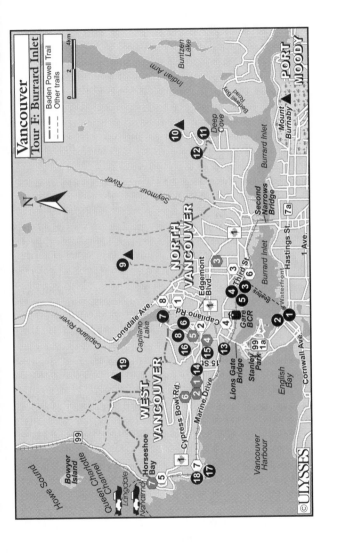

and the mountains as well as all the activity at the nearby port with the colourful tugboat dock flanking the market to the east. Built in 1986, Lonsdale Quay Market was the brainchild of architects Hotson and Bakker who wanted to satisfy every basic human need here: food (ground floor), clothing (second floor) and lodging (upper floors, p 147). From here, Vancouver really looks like a Manhattan in the making.

The market is the main urban attraction in North Vancouver, a suburb of 68,000 people sandwiched between Burrard Inlet and mountains over 1,500m high. The urbanization of the north shore of the inlet began in the second half of the 19th century. Some businessmen from New Westminster decided to make capital of the firs, hemlock spruce and red cedars in the surrounding forest. It was Maine (U.S.) native Sewell Prescott Moody, however, who made British Columbia's wood known around the world. Ferry service between Gastown (see p 66) and "his" town, Moodyville, was introduced in 1866. At the beginning of the 20th century, most of the property in North and West Vancouver was transferred to British interests who began developing the areas as residential suburbs.

North of the market, you can enjoy a pleasant stroll along Lonsdale Avenue. The old banks and public buildings bear witness to the prosperous past of the wood industry. Keep walking until you reach Victoria Park, then head west on Sixth Street to return to Burrard Inlet. On either side of the market, the east shore is scattered with tiny Aboriginal reserves, some barely two blocks across. One of these is the **Mission Indian Reserve**, centred around Mission Road, which leads to West Esplanade. There you will find the **St. Paul Catholic Church**, erected between 1884 and 1909 by Oblate missionaries from Quebec. The interior is decorated with stained-glass windows and polychrome statues.

If you are travelling by car, return to Marine Drive heading west and go up Capilano Road until you reach the **Capilano Suspension Bridge and Park** (*$10; May to Oct 8am to 9pm; Nov to Apr 9am to 5pm; 3735 Capilano Rd.,* ☎*985-7474*). If you are on foot at Lonsdale Quay Market, take bus number 236 to Edgmont Boulevard. Paths lead to this metal-cabled bridge, suspended 70m above the Capilano River, which replaced the original bridge of rope and wood built in 1899. The presence of indigenous peoples is more evident in

British Columbian society than in any other Canadian province. Many gather in this park each summer to carve totem poles.

Three kilometres to the north is the **Capilano Fish Hatchery ★** *(free entry; 4500 Capilano Park Rd., ☎666-1790)*, the first salmon hatchery in British Columbia. This well laid-out spot provides visitors with an introduction to the life cycle of the salmon.

In the summer, Pacific salmon wear themselves out as they make their way up the Capilano River to reach their spawning grounds, making for an exceptional spectacle for visitors.

The upper part of Upper Capilano Road was renamed Nancy Greene Way after the Canadian skier who won the gold medal for the giant slalom at the 1968 Olympics in Grenoble, France. On the left, a road leads to **Cleveland Dam Park ★★** on the shores of Lake Capilano. The construction in 1954 of the impressive 100m-high dam at the centre of the park led to the creation of the lake,

Vancouver's main source of drinking water. Spectacular views of the neighbouring mountains surround the park.

At the north end of Nancy Greene Way, there is a **cable car** *($17; summer every day 9am to 10pm, Sat and Sun 8am to 10pm; ☎984-0661)* that carries passengers to the top of **Grouse Mountain ★★★** where, at an altitude of 1,250m, skiers and hikers can contemplate the entire Vancouver area as well as Washington State (in clear weather) to the south. The view is particularly beautiful at the end of the day. Wilderness trails lead out from the various viewing areas. During summer, Grouse Mountain is also a popular spot for hang-gliding.

Among the other sights in North Vancouver that are accessible by car and worth mentioning is **Mount Seymour Provincial Park ★★** *(Mount Seymour Parkway)* where skiing is possible both day and night. There are also a number of cross-country trails that become hiking paths in the summer. **Deep Cove**, at the eastern edge of North Vancouver on the shore of Indian Arm, is a fine spot for canoeing and kayaking. Close to the vil-

Exploring

lage is the head of the **Baden Powell Trail** ★★ which runs through the wilderness all the way to Horseshoe Bay, 42km to the west.

The Burrard Inlet walking tour ends at Grouse Mountain.

To return to Vancouver, get on the bus again, then take the Seabus back the other way. Motorists can continue exploring the area by heading to **West Vancouver** ★★ *(go back down Upper Capilano Rd., then turn right on Marine Dr.)*, a fashionable residential suburb located on a mountainside. Many talented architects have helped enrich the city's modern heritage.

Marine Drive leads past two large shopping centres. On Marine Drive between 24th and 25th Streets is another charming shopping area called Dundarave. **Ambleside Park** ★, located to their west, is worth a stop since it offers some lovely views of Stanley Park and Lions Gate Bridge. Near the water, landscape architect Don Vaughan created the **Waterside Fountain** out of cubes of granite in 1989. West of the park, an attractive promenade leads along the water to 24th Street.

Turn right on 15th Street, then right again on Lawson Avenue where you'll find

Pratt House *(1460 Lawson Ave.; not open to the public)*, designed by architect C.E. Pratt in 1948 for his own use. Pratt was a great promoter of this style of wooden house, which is open on the outside and blends into the natural environment. Although designed to withstand earthquakes and resist rotting due to the heavy rainfall here (wide-edged roofs, cedar construction), these houses might appear fragile to Europeans more accustomed to stone and brick buildings.

The nearby **Berwick House** *(1650 Mathers Ave.; not open to the public)*, designed by the same architect, dates back to 1939. It was thus a forerunner of this type of construction. Since the 1930s, Canadian architects working on the West Coast have been greatly influenced both by the Californian buildings of the Greene brothers and Richard Neutra as well as by much older Japanese designs dating from the time of the *shoguns*.

Head north on 15th Street, which becomes Cross Creek Road, and then Eyremount Drive.

Next, you'll reach **British Properties** ★ *(on either side of the road starting at Highland Dr.)*, where untouched woodlands and suburbia overlap. British Pacific Properties Limited, owned by London's famous Guinness family known for their stout, began developing this mountainous area in 1932. The overall design was the work of the Olmsted Brothers, the worthy successors of Frederick Law Olmsted whose credits include Montreal's Mount Royal Park and New York's Central Park.

Return to Marine Drive.

Turn right on Marine Drive and continue to **Lighthouse Park ★** *(entrance on Beacon Lane)*, located on a point that stretches out into the Strait of Georgia and has a lighthouse on its southern tip. Strolling around this peaceful place truly evokes a feeling of infinite space. The nearby **Gordon Smith House** *(The Byway via Howe Sound Lane; not open to the public)* is a West Coast version of the glass houses of Mies van der Rohe and Philip Jonson. Designed by Erickson and Massey, it was built in 1965. Arthur Erickson, also mentioned in the previous tours, also designed the Canadian Embassy in Washington D.C.

Like the Trans-Canada Highway, Marine Drive ends at the port of the village of **Horseshoe Bay ★** where the terminal for the ferry to Vancouver Island is located. To return to Vancouver, head east on the Trans-Canada Highway, then follow the signs for Lions Gate Bridge. On the way, there is an exit for **Cypress Bowl Road**, a scenic road whose steep hills are ill-suited to cars with weak engines. It leads to **Cypress Park ★★★** and Cypress Bowl itself, a mountain where skiers can enjoy a 900m vertical drop and breathtaking views of the Strait of Georgia.

Tour G: False Creek

False Creek is located south of downtown Vancouver and, like Burrard Inlet, stretches far inland. The presence of both water and a railroad induced a large number of sawmills to set up shop in this area in the early 20th century.

These mills gradually filled a portion of False Creek, leaving only a narrow channel to provide them with water which is necessary for sawing. Over the years, two thirds of False Creek, as explorer George Vancouver had known it in 1790, disappeared under asphalt.

In 1974, when the local sawmills shut down en masse, people began moving into new housing developments, the likes of which

Exploring

were becoming more and more popular around the world by that time. Then, in 1986, False Creek hosted Expo '86, attracting several million visitors here in the space of a few months.

Get off at the Skytrain's Main Street Station, located opposite the long Beaux-Arts facade of **Pacific Central Station** *(1150 Station St.).* Determined not to be out-done, Canadian National (formerly the Canadian Northern Pacific Railway Company) copied Canadian Pacific by building a second transcontinental railway. It ran parallel to the first and ended at this station, erected in 1919 on the em-bankment of False Creek. Today, it welcomes Cana-dian VIA trains and U.S. Amtrak trains as well as various private trains which use the tracks running

through the Rockies for scenic tours.

Head over to **Science World ★** *($11.75 or $14.75 with movie; 1455 Quebec St., ☎443-7440),* the big silver ball at the end of False Creek. Architect Bruno Freschi designed this 14-storey building as a wel-come centre for visitors to Expo '86. It was the only pavilion built to remain in place after the big event. The sphere representing the Earth has supplanted the tower as the quintessential symbol of these fairs since Expo '67 in Montréal. Van-couver's sphere contains an Omnimax theatre which presents films on a giant, dome-shaped screen. The rest of the building is now occupied by a museum that explores the secrets of sci-ence from all different an-gles.

● ATTRACTIONS	● RESTAURANTS
1. Pacific Central Station	1. Bin 941
2. Science World	2. Bridges Bistro
3. GM Place	3. C
4. BC Place Stadium	4. Château Madrid - La Bodega
5. Concord Pacific Place	5. Étoile
6. Concord Pacific Place Presentation Centre	6. Il Giardino
7. CPR Roundhouse	7. Kamei Royale Ocean
8. Vancouver Aquatic Centre	8. Kittle of fish
9. Granville Island & Public Market	9. La Baguette et l'Échalote
10. Emily Carr College of Art and Design	10. Monk McQueen's
11. Granville Island Brewing Company	11. Pacific Institut of Culinary Arts
12. Granville Island Sport Fishing Museum	12. Panama Jacks Bar & Grill
13. False Creek Development	13. The Creek Restaurant & Brewery
14. False Creek Park	14. The Keg

Due to the massive influx of Asian immigrants, Vancouver's Chinatown has become one of the largest in North America.
- *P. Brunet*

English Bay Beach, whose sands are a short distance from the heart Vancouver, is it with urban beach-goers.
Tibor Bognàr

Stanley Park is proof positive that despite Vancouver's many skyscrap the city maintains close ties with the nearby wilderness. - *Sheila Nain*

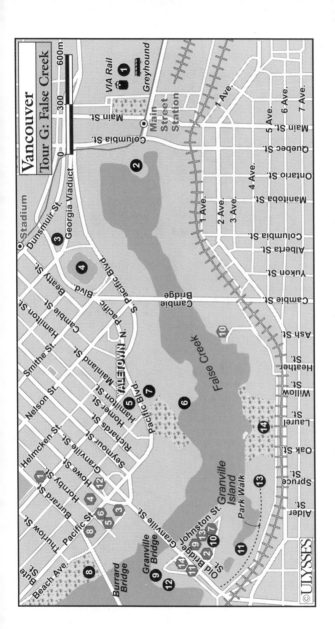

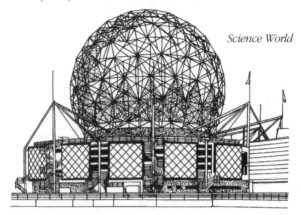

Science World

Walk alongside False Creek to Pacific Boulevard South before plunging into the void beneath Cambie Bridge.

During the summer of 1986, the vast stretch of unused land along the north shore of False Creek was occupied by dozens of showy pavilions with visitors crowding around them. Visible on the other side of an access road, **GM Place** *(Pacific Blvd. at the corner of Abbott, ☎899-7400)* is a 20,000-seat amphitheatre that was completed in 1995 and now hosts the home games of the local hockey and basketball teams, the Vancouver Canucks and Grizzlies respectively. Its big brother, **BC Place Stadium** *(777 Pacific Blvd. N., ☎669-2300, 661-7373 or 661-2122, ≈661-3412)* stands to the south. Its 60,000 seats are highly coveted by fans of Canadian football who come here to cheer on the

B.C. Lions. Big trade fairs and rock concerts are also held in the stadium.

Development of the grounds of Expo '86 has made good progress due to the city's thriving economy and thanks to the capital that flowed out of Hong Kong on the eve of the British colony's return to communist China in 1997. Plans are underway to build high-rises containing thousands of apartments flanked by gardens similar to those in the West End. The first phase of the project known as **Concord Pacific Place**, named after a major Hong Kong real-estate developer, was completed in 1994. The high-rises, whose architecture resembles that of Battery Park City in New York, line Pacific Boulevard between Homer and Cambie Streets. A model of the entire project is on display at the **Concord Pacific Place Pre-**

sentation Centre on the waterfront.

The beautifully restored **CPR Roundhouse ★** *(at the corner of Davie St. and Pacific Blvd.)*, located opposite, is all that remains of the Canadian Pacific marshalling yard once located on this site. Erected in 1888, it was used for the servicing and repair of locomotives. Granville Island is visible across the water, as are the new residential areas along False Creek.

Follow Pacific Boulevard under Granville Bridge, then turn left on Hornby Street and right on Beach Avenue. This will lead you to the **Vancouver Aquatic Centre** *(☎665-4324)*, a large indoor public pool and gym located on the other side of the Burrard Street Bridge.

Follow Pacific Boulevard under Granville Bridge, then turn left on Hornby Street and right on Beach Avenue. The False Creek ferry docks are nearby; catch a ferry for **Granville Island and its public market ★★**. You'll notice the vaguely Art Deco pillars of the Burrard Street Bridge (1930). In 1977, this artificial island, created in 1914 and once used for industrial purposes, saw its warehouses and factories transformed into a major recreational and commercial

centre. The area has since come to life thanks to a revitalization project. A public market, many shops and all sorts of restaurants, plus theatres and artists' studios are all part of Granville Island. You will also find a community centre and the **Emily Carr College of Art and Design** which was enlarged considerably in 1996 and presents exhibitions of work by students and various artists from British Columbia. Not to be missed on the island is the micro-brewery tour offered by the **Granville Island Brewing Company** *(summer, Mon to Thu 9:30am to 7pm, Fri and Sat to 8pm; guided tours $6, summer every day noon to 5pm on the hour; winter every day, call ahead for store and tour schedules; 1441 Cartwright St., ☎687-BREW)*. The newly renovated facilities, opened in late May 1997 include a specialty beer and wine store, a tasting-room and a brewhouse. Avoid taking your car onto the island; traffic jams are common and parking is hard to find. To reach the island without following the False Creek tour, take bus number 50 heading south from Howe Street downtown.

On the island, take Anderson Street south alongside Granville Bridge, then turn left on Park Walk.

Exploring

Granville Island Sport Fishing Museum *(1502 Duranleau, Granville Island, ☎683-1939).* This museum boasts an international collection of artifacts – some very old – all related to sport fishing in British Columbia. It is situated in the heart of Granville Island, a stone's throw from the large covered market. The exhibits dedicated to fly-fishing are very impressive. Here you will enter a fascinating world, one full of rituals where ecology and entomology is a prerequisite to knowledge of successful fly-fishing. Once you have caught the "bug" after visiting this lovely museum, you will have the urge to equip yourselves and head for the great outdoors. The museum's information centre offers a complete list of outfitters, lodges, clubs and the best fishing spots in British Columbia.

You will now enter the **False Creek Development ★**, a residential area begun in 1974 and built in stages by private developers on formerly polluted government land. It is pleasant to wander about on the pedestrian walkways around **False Creek Park** and look at the carefully designed groups of houses.

Tour H: Shaughnessy and South Vancouver

This tour covers two separate neighbourhoods located south of False Creek, the City Hall area and the Shaughnessy Heights area.

In the 1930s, the municipal government planned to make the first area of this tour Vancouver's new downtown core in an effort to shift the city centre. This involved building a new city hall near Broadway. It is true that when you look at a map, you realize that Vancouver's business section is located at the northern edge of town, on a peninsula accessible mainly by bridges. Practical as it was, however, the project was a bitter failure, as illustrated by the solitary tower of City Hall, rising up amidst scores of cottage-style houses.

Shaughnessy Heights, the second area, is an affluent residential enclave laid out by Canadian Pacific starting in 1907. It succeeded the West End as a refuge for well-heeled Vancouverites. The area was named after Thomas G. Shaughnessy who was then president of C.P.

Vancouver
Tour H: Shaughnessy

N

Pacific Blvd.
Granville St. Bridge
Granville Island
False Creek
Cambie Bridge
Main Street Station
Terminal Ave.

FAIRVIEW
6 Ave.
7 Ave.
8 Ave.
Broadway
10 Ave.
12 Ave.
14 Ave.
15 Ave.

MOUNT PLEASANT
1 Ave.
2 Ave.
3 Ave.
5 Ave.
6 Ave.
7 Ave.
6th Ave.
Broadway
12 Ave.
14 Ave.
15 Ave.
16 Ave.

Vancouver General Hospital

The Crescent
SHAUGHNESSY
17 Ave.
18 Ave.
16 Ave.
18 Ave.
20 Ave.
21 Ave.
23 Ave.
24 Ave.

King Edward Ave.
CAMBIE
26 Ave.
27 Ave.
28 Ave.

Grace and Children's Hospital
33 Ave.
37 Ave.
41 Ave.

FRASER
31 Ave.
33 Ave.
37 Ave.
39 Ave.
40 Ave.
MAIN

Granville St. Bridge, Connaught Dr., Alexandra St., Cartier St., Hudson St., Selkirk St., Osler St., Oak St., Granville St., Devonshire Dr., Heather St., Laurel St., Willow St., Heather St., Tupper St., Ash St., Cambie St., Yukon St., Columbia St., Manitoba St., Ontario St., Main St., Fraser St., Prince Edward St., Kingsway, Midlothian

0   500   1000m

©ULYSSES

● ATTRACTIONS

1. City Hall
2. Vancouver General Hospital
3. Walter C. Nichol House
4. McRae House
5. Van Dusen Botanical Gardens
6. Queen Elizabeth Park

○ ACCOMMODATIONS

1. Pillow Porridge Guest House
2. Plaza 500 Hotel
3. Ramada Vancouver Centre

● RESTAURANTS

1. Amourous Oyster
2. Big News Coffee Bar
3. Landmark Hotpot House
4. Ohana Sushi
5. Royal Seoul House Korean Restaurant

He also lived in the house of the same name in Montreal that is now part of the Canadian Centre for Architecture. A number of local streets, furthermore, were named after the eminent families of Montreal's Golden Square Mile, like the Hosmers, the Oslers and the Anguses.

The tour starts at the corner of Cambie and Broadway.

Head south on Cambie Street to **City Hall** *(453 West 12th Ave.)*, a massive, austere-looking tower topped by public clocks and featuring both classical and Art Deco elements (1935).

Head west on 12th Avenue.

Next, you will pass **Vancouver General Hospital** *(855 West 12th Ave.)*, one of the largest hospitals in North America. Several of its buildings were erected in the Streamline Deco style between 1944 and 1950. Unlike the geometric, vertical Art Deco style, the Streamline Deco or "steamship" style features rounded, horizontal lines which symbolize speed and modernism.

Turn left on Oak Street, then right on 16th Ave.

Take Tecumseh Avenue into Shaughnessy Heights and walk around The Crescent to get a taste of the opulence of the houses in this area. Of all the houses, the most elegant is definitely **Walter C. Nichol House** ★ *(1402 The Crescent; not open to the public)*, a masterpiece by Maclure and Fox that was built in 1912 for the former Lieutenant Governor of British Columbia. The half-timbering and mullioned windows typical of English farms and manors are clear reminders of the British roots that characterize this province despite its great distance from the mother country.

Typical Shaughnessy House

Furthermore, as the climate is similar to that of England, these houses boast front gardens as lovely as those found on the outskirts of London.

Steal along McRae Avenue where you'll find the largest

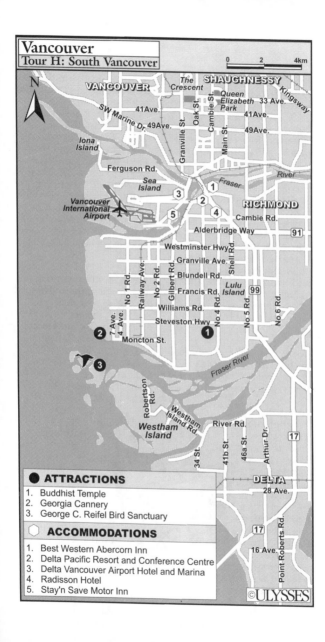

Vancouver
Tour H: South Vancouver

0 2 4km

N

VANCOUVER

The Crescent

SHAUGHNESSY

SW Marine Dr. 41 Ave.

49 Ave.

Granville St.

Oak St.

Cambie St.

Main St.

Queen Elizabeth Park

33 Ave.

41 Ave.

49 Ave.

Kingsway

Iona Island

Ferguson Rd.

Sea Island

Vancouver International Airport

Fraser River

RICHMOND

③

①

②

④

⑤

Cambie Rd.

Alderbridge Way

91

Westminster Hwy.

Granville Ave.

Blundell Rd.

Francis Rd.

Shell Rd.

Gilbert Rd.

No 1 Rd.

Railway Ave.

No 2 Rd.

Lulu Island

99

Williams Rd.

Steveston Hwy.

No 4 Rd.

No 5 Rd.

No 6 Rd.

② 7 Ave.
4 Ave.

Moncton St.

● ①

● ③

Fraser River

Robertson Rd.

Westham Island Rd.

Westham Island

River Rd.

34 St.

41b St.

46a St.

Arthur Dr.

17

DELTA

28 Ave.

17

16 Ave.

Point Roberts Rd.

● ATTRACTIONS
1. Buddhist Temple
2. Georgia Cannery
3. George C. Reifel Bird Sanctuary

◯ ACCOMMODATIONS
1. Best Western Abercorn Inn
2. Delta Pacific Resort and Conference Centre
3. Delta Vancouver Airport Hotel and Marina
4. Radisson Hotel
5. Stay'n Save Motor Inn

©ULYSSES

home in Shaughnessy Heights, **McRae House** ★ *(1489 McRae Ave.)*, also known as Hycroft. Built in 1909 for General Alexander McRae, it was designed by Thomas Hooper. The long façade has a projecting portico in the Beaux Arts spirit. The interior, decorated by Charles Marega, who sculpted the lions for Lions Gate Bridge, boldly combines Italian rococo with English neoclassicism. Like many other mansions across Canada, McRae House was abandoned by its owners and liveried servants after the stock market crash of 1929. Since 1961, it has been occupied by the University Women's Club.

Go back and complete the loop of The Crescent, then take Osler Avenue southward out of Shaughnessy Heights.

Turn left on 33rd Avenue, then right on Oak Street where you'll find the entrance to the **Van Dusen Botanical Gardens** ★★ *(summer $5.50, winter $2.75; every day, summer 10am to nightfall, call for exact schedule; Apr and Sep 10am to 6pm; Oct to Mar 10am to 4pm; free guided tours every day, 1pm, 2pm and 3pm; 5251 Oak St., ☎878-9274).* Since Vancou-

ver is so blessed by Mother Nature, a number of lovely gardens have been planted in the area, including this one which boasts plant species from all over the world. When the rhododendrons are in bloom (late May), the garden deserves another star. At the far end is a housing co-op that blends in so perfectly with the greenery that it looks like a gigantic ornamental sculpture (McCarter, Nairne and Associates, 1976).

Further east on 33rd Avenue is another magnificent green space, **Queen Elizabeth Park** ★★ *(corner of 33rd Ave. and Cambie St.)*, laid out around the **Bloedel Floral Conservatory** *($3.50; Apr to Sep, Mon to Fri 9am to 8pm, Sat and Sun 10am to 9pm; Oct to Mar, every day 10am to 5pm; at the top of Queen Elizabeth Park, ☎257-8570).* The latter, shaped like an overturned glass saucer, houses exotic plants and birds. The Bloedel company, which sponsored the conservatory, is the principal lumber company in British Columbia. This park's rhododendron bushes also merit a visit in springtime. Finally, the outdoor gardens offer a spectacular view of the city, English Bay and the surrounding mountains.

The walking tour ends here. Catch bus #15 on Cambie Street to go back downtown.

One of the other attractions in South Vancouver that visitors with cars can visit is the second biggest **Buddhist temple in North America** *(every day 10am to 5pm; 9160 Steveston Hwy., Richmond, ☎274-2822)*. To get there, take Oak Street southward toward Highway 99, which leads to the ferry for Victoria, and get off at the Steveston Highway West exit. Located between the third and fourth streets on your left, this place of worship has free entry.

Get back on the Steveston Highway heading west, turn left on Fourth Avenue, and continue to the end of this avenue. The **Georgia Cannery** ★ *($5; Jul and Aug, every day 10am to 5pm; May, Jun and Sep, Thu to Mon 10am to 5pm; guided tours every hour; 12138 Fourth Ave., Richmond, ☎664-9009)*, restored by Parks Canada, retraces the history of the fishing industry in Steveston. This historic spot explains the steps involved in conserving fish, especially salmon, and also shows how herring is transformed into pet food and oil. Very interesting. Leaving this establishment, stay along the seashore by way of the wooden walkway near the fishing boats. Fishing remains an important

economic activity in this region. A commercial area with restaurants and shops invites you to relax. The day's catch is served in the restaurants.

Turn back along the Steveston Highway, this time heading east, and take Route 99 toward the ferry pier for Victoria; take the Ladner exit after the tunnel. Go along this road and follow the signs to the **George C. Reifel Bird Sanctuary** ★★ *($3.25; every day 9am to 4pm, 5191 Robertson Rd., Delta, ☎946-6980)*. Each year more than 350 species of birds visit this magical spot in the marshlands at the mouth of the Fraser River.

Tour I: The West Side

The culture of the Pacific as well as the history and traditions of the Aboriginal peoples are omnipresent throughout this tour that follows the shore of the vast peninsula that is home to the majority of Vancouver's residents. Posh residential neighbourhoods, numerous museums, a university campus and several sand and quartz beaches from which Vancouver Island is visible on a clear day all make up this tour.

Exploring

● ATTRACTIONS

1. Vanier Park
2. Tatlow Court
3. Pioneer Park
4. Jericho Beach Park
5. Point Grey
6. University of British Columbia
7. Museum of Anthropology
8. Asian Centre
9. First Nations House of Learning
10. Wreck Beach

◐ ACCOMMODATIONS

1. Penny Farthing Inn Bed & Breakfast
2. The Johnson House Bed & Breakfast
3. UBC Housing and Conference Center
4. Vancouver International Hostel

● RESTAURANTS

1. Bino's
2. Bread Garden
3. De Dutch Pannekoek House
4. Epicurean Caffe
5. Fiction
6. Flying Wedge Pizza Co.
7. Gypsy Rose
8. Japanese Bistro Kitsilano
9. Las Margaritas
10 Lumière
11. Maria's Taverna
12. Mark's Steak and Tap House
13. Ouisi Bistro
14. Pâtisserie Lebeau
15. Primo's Mexicain Grill
16. Raku Kushiyaki Restaurant
17. Sienna Tapas Bar & Grill
18. Sophie's Cosmic Café
19. Star Anise
20. The Naam
21. The Smoking Dog
22. The Vineyard

This is a driving tour, as it extends over 15km. The first four attractions are accessible aboard bus # 22 from downtown or by taking bus # 4 directly the University of British Columbia campus.

Exit the downtown area by the Burrard Street Bridge.

Keep right, and immediately after going down the roadway leading off the bridge, take a right on Chestnut Street to get to **Vanier Park** which is home to three museums.

The **Vancouver Museum** ★★ *($8; Jul and Aug, every day 10am to 5pm; Sep to June closed Mon; 1100 Chestnut St., in Vanier Park,* ☎736-4431) forms its centrepiece. This museum, whose dome resembles the head-dress worn by the coast Salish First Nation, presents exhibitions on the history of the different peoples who have inhabited the region.

On the same spot is the **Pacific Space Centre** *($12.50; presentations Tue to Sun 2:30pm and 8pm, extra shows Sat and Sun 1pm and 4pm;* ☎738-7827), which houses

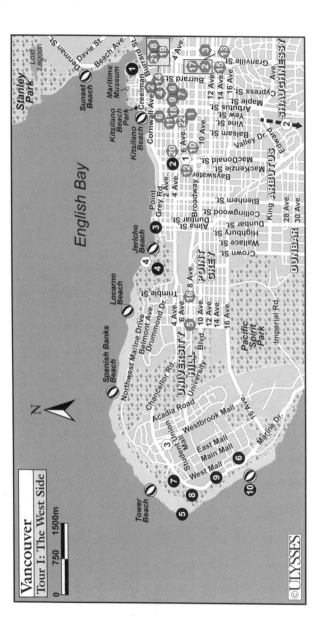

the H.R. MacMillan Planetarium and relates the creation of the universe. It has a telescope through which you can admire the stars. The **Maritime Museum** *($6; May to Oct, every day 10am to 5pm; Nov to Apr closed Mon; 1905 Ogden Ave., ☎257-8300)* completes the trio of institutions in Vanier Park. Being a major seaport, it is only natural that Vancouver should have its own maritime museum. The key attraction is the *Saint-Roch*, the first boat to circle North America by navigating the Panamá Canal and the Northwest Passage.

Get back on Chestnut Street and turn right on Cornwall Avenue, which becomes a scenic road named Point Grey Road.

You will now pass through **Kitsilano** *(between Arbutus and Alma Sts.)*, bordered to the north by a public beach. This area, whose wooden Queen Anne and Western Bungalow Style houses are typical of the West Coast, was a middle-class neighbourhood in the early 20th century. If you want to leave no stone unturned during your tour of Kitsilano, take a left on MacDonald Street. Around number 2100, a lovely row of gabled houses, each with a veranda in front, forms a cohesive whole. They date back to 1912.

Turn right on Sixth Avenue, then right again on Bayswater Street.

Tatlow Court *(1820 Bayswater St.)*, a group of neo-Tudor row houses built around a central court, is worth a quick look.

Turn left on Point Grey Road, then right on Alma Street, which leads to **Pioneer Park**, home of the **Hasting Mills Store** *(1575 Alma St.)*. Built in 1865, this former general store is the oldest building in Vancouver. Originally located east of Gastown, near the city's first sawmill, it was transported here by boat in 1930 and then restored by the Native Daughters of British Columbia, a charitable organization which, in spite of its name, has nothing to do with indigenous peoples.

Head south on Alma Street, then turn right on Fourth Avenue.

Fourth Avenue runs alongside lovely **Jericho Beach Park**, a green space and beach rolled into one at the edge of English Bay. Turn right on Northwest Marine Drive, then left on Belmont Avenue to see some of the loveliest houses on the peninsula. Return to Northwest Marine Drive and head west to **Point Grey** ★★★, also known as Pacific Spirit Park. It stretches out into the salt water, offering a full panoramic view of the Strait of Georgia.

The tour continues onto the grounds of the **University of British Columbia ★**, or UBC. The university was created by the provincial government in 1908, but it was not until 1925 that the campus opened its doors on this lovely site on Point Grey. An architectural contest had been organized for the site layout, but the First World War halted construction work. It took a student demonstration denouncing government inaction on this matter to get the buildings completed. Only the library and the science building were executed according to the original plans. **Set Foot for UBC** *(May to Aug, free tours organized by students,* ☎*822-TOUR).*

To this day, the UBC campus is constantly expanding, so don't be surprised by its somewhat heterogeneous appearance. There are, however, a few gems however, including the **Museum of Anthropology ★★★** *($6, free admission Tue 5pm to 9pm; in the summer, every day 10am to 5pm, in the winter closed Mon and Dec 25 and 26; 6393 NW Marine Dr.; from downtown, take bus #4 UBC or bus #10 UBC;* ☎*822-3825).* It's not to be missed both for the quality of Aboriginal artwork displayed here,

including totem poles, and for the architecture of Arthur Erickson. Big concrete beams and columns imitate the shapes of traditional Aboriginal houses, beneath which have been erected immense totem poles gathered from former Aboriginal villages along the coast and on the islands. Wooden sculptures and various works of art form part of the permanent exhibition.

On the edge of the West Mall is the **Asian Centre** *(1871 West Mall)* that is capped with a big pyramid-shaped metal roof. It houses the department of Asian studies and an exhibition centre. Behind the building is the magnificent **Nitobe Memorial Garden ★★** *($4.50 summer, free winter, mid-Mar to mid-Oct, every day 10am to 6pm; winter, Mon to Fri 10am to 2:30pm;* ☎*822-9666)* which symbolically faces Japan on the other side of the Pacific. Further along, **First Nations House of Learning ★** is a community centre for Aboriginal students that was completed in 1993. It was designed to be a modern version of a Coast Salish Longhouse. The curved roof evokes the spirit of a bird (Larry Macfarland, architect). Totem poles surround the great hall that can accommodate up to 400 people at a time.

The southwestern edge of the campus harbours a spot

Exploring

unlike any other – **Wreck Beach** ★ *(NW Marine Dr. at University St.)* – where students come to enjoy some of life's pleasures. Nudists have made this their refuge, as have sculptors, who exhibit their talents on large pieces of driftwood. Vendors hawk all sorts of items next to improvised fast-food stands. A long stairway, quite steep in places, leads down to the beach.

Excursions Outside Vancouver

Among the many reasons to appreciate Vancouver, one in particular stands out. Unlike certain cities, where nearby suburbs are often the only place to get away for the weekend, Vancouver offers a wide choice of nearby destinations: **Whistler**, **Vancouver Island** and the **Gulf Islands** are the most famous.

Whistler (one day)

Whistler and **Blackcomb Mountains** *(hotel reservations: ☎932-4222, from Vancouver ☎685-3650, from the US ☎800-634-9622)* together make up the largest skiing area in Canada. As previously mentioned, these mountains have much to offer in the winter (see p 135 in "Outdoor Activities").

In the summer, a one day excursion to Whistler can also be very pleasant with its countless boutiques and restaurants. Prices are, however, sometimes high. A place for hat lovers, **The Hat Gallery** *(☎938-6695)* sells local creations and receives orders from as far away as Switzerland. Come nightfall, the town rocks to rhythms emanating from a dozen nightclubs. In the summer, the Vancouver Symphony Orchestra plays at the top of **Whistler Mountain** *(☎932-3434)* in the midst of unbelievable scenery.

Getting To Whistler

By train: with **B.C. Rail** *(in Vancouver, ☎984-5246)* from North Vancouver.
By bus: **Greyhound** *(☎800-667-0882)* offers several daily departures from Vancouver.
By car: via **Highway 99 North**. Vancouver: 120km, 2hrs 15min; Kamloops: 400km, 5.5hrs; Seattle, WA: 338km, 5hrs.

Vancouver Island

Victoria (one to two days)

Victoria is a very British city. Many symbols from old England give it a particularly captivating charm. Anglophiles and the British

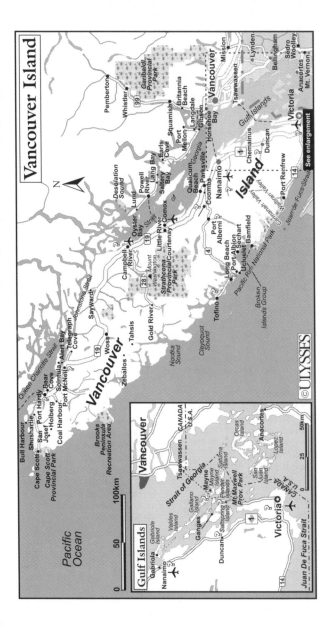

will feel at home walking along **Government Street** and the **Port**. Buildings from the beginning of the century confer a particular style to this modern city. Among these are the **Parliament Buildings** and the shops, the most characteristic of which is the Morris Tobacconist Store where you can still light up a cigar just like in the good old days. For the ultimate British experience, visitors can have tea in the majestic setting of the **Empress Hotel** (☎250-384-8111). Reservations are recommended. Victoria's historic charm is further emphasized by its numerous buildings by the water, actually listed as historic monuments, such as the **Market Square** which houses 40 original and colourful boutiques. Nearby, **Chinatown** has chosen this 19th-century district with winding alleys to set up its restaurants and shops. Victoria is not only nostalgic. Besides the tattoo shops and health food stores, its development and "hippie-environmentalist" influence have spawned cybercafés like the **Mocambo Café** (☎250-384-4468) where everyone surfs the Net at their leisure. A touch esoteric, local art is notably displayed at the **MacPherson Theatre** and the **Art Gallery of Greater Victoria**. Tarot-card fans can meet specialized readers at the **Avallon Meta-physical Centre** (☎250-380-1721). Victoria is one of the loveliest seaside cities. A stroll along **Dallas Sunken Road** and **Beach Drive** is highly recommended. Here, opulent houses graced with gardens rival small rocky cliffs, and the view of the **Juan de Fuca Strait** is simply magnificent. To the north, the towns of **Oak Bay** and **Cadboro Bay** offer beautiful scenery along the beaches. Twenty minutes outside of Victoria is the enchanting countryside where a series of flowerbeds dot the landscape. You can make the most of it by having a picnic in **John Dean Park**, but the best-known place in town remains world-famous **Butchart Gardens** (☎250-652-5256).

South Coast (one day)

Vancouver Island's south coast is studded with local art boutiques. Nature's influence is notably apparent in all forms of art here, including numerous sculptures and paintings by First Nations artists. By going through **Duncan**, you can visit the **Cowichan Native Village** (☎250-746-8119). The guided tour illustrates the way of life of Aboriginal people, their customs and buildings. A very beautiful film is also presented, and an art gallery and totem poles allow visitors to learn more about Aboriginal art.

In **Qualicum Beach**, the **Brant Festival** (*☎250-248-4117*) marks the return of thousands of geese in April. Further north, Campbell River lures steelhead and salmon fishing buffs.

West Coast

On the island's west coast, the hundred-year-old temperate rain forests and beaches skirting the cliffs are frequented by amateur and professional naturalists alike. Whale-watching excursions leave from Tofino. In Long Beach, waves crest as high as 8m in the winter along the spectacular 15km-long beach. Dedicated hikers will enjoy the **West Coast Trail**, in the **Pacific Rim National Park**, which takes from five to seven days to cover (*reservations required, ☎663-6000 from Vancouver*). Other hidden ecological treasures on this island include: the **Carmanah Valley**, a forest of giant thousand-year old trees; the wild fjord of **Clayoquot Sound** and **Walbran Valley** (*B.C. Parks: ☎250-387-5002*); and a new provincial park where old Sitka spruce trees stand almost 100m tall. For further details, contact **Tourism Victoria** (*☎800-663-3883*) or the **Tourism Association of Vancouver Island** (*☎250-382-3551*).

Getting to Vancouver Island

B.C. Ferries (*☎888-223-3779 in BC, out of province: 250-386-3431*) offer several daily departures from Tsawwassen and Horseshoe Bay. By seaplane, **Air B.C.** (*Vancouver, ☎688-5515*) and **Harbour Air** (*☎800-663-4267*) fly from one downtown area to another. By helicopter, **Helijet** (*Vancouver, ☎273-1414*) also provides transportation to this area.

The Gulf Islands (two to four days)

These natural islands have retained their wild essence and charm by not being overly commercially developed; no concrete and few cars mar their beauty. These islands constitute havens of peace for stressed-out Vancouverites and hippies alike.

Salt Spring Island

With many art galleries, restaurants and boutiques, Salt Spring is the most touristy of the Gulf Islands. During the summer, artists and artisans flood the streets, exhibiting their work. Throughout the island, "Studio" signs line the streets, indicating that is it possible to visit artists in their studios.

Exploring

Salt Spring Island boasts over 75 bed and breakfasts, hotels and log cabins by the water. For further details, contact the **Salt Spring Island Visitor Information Centre** (☎250-537-5252).

Mayne Island

Unlike Salt Spring, Mayne does nothing to court tourists. Roadsigns are virtually non-existent. It is therefore recommended that you study the only public road map set up near the harbour. Only a few remaining historic buildings testify to the island's past role as a prison; then it was nicknamed Little Hell. Relics confirm the island was once a colonial outpost with old trading posts and shops; the old **Mayne Inn Hotel** (☎250-539-3122), with its period architecture, remains intact. For provisions and camping or hiking gear, **Miners Trading Post** (☎250-539-2214), in the village of **Fernhill**, is a good bet. You can purchase tasty organic fruits and vegetables at the **Mayne Open Market** (☎250-539-5024), locally known as MOM. The **Arbutus Deer Farm** (☎250-539-2301) sells venison and beef for barbecues. **Bennett Bay Beach** is a lovely place for a stroll. Both **Pacific Spirit Air** (☎800-665-2359) and **Harbour Air** (☎800-665-0212) offer direct flights between Vancouver and Mayne Island.

Pender Islands

Linked by a wooden bridge, the two Pender Islands, much like Mayne, are very quiet and their inhabitants don't like to be disturbed. Visitors come here especially to go bike riding and stroll along the long stretch of **beaches**. Mount Normand has a good reputation among hikers. The summit offers a unique view of the San Juan Islands. The "hippie-cool" ambiance of these islands is obvious; natural food stores and organic produce farms prevail here. Try the **Southridge Farms Country Store** (☎250-629-2051) for organic fruits and vegetables. Sample excellent cuisine at the **Bedwell** restaurant (☎250-629-3212) or enjoy a beer at the **Port Browning Marina** pub (☎250-629-3493) where local musicians often get together for jam nights. Bed and breakfasts ensure accommodation. For further information, write to the **South Pender Island B & B** (9956 Boundary Pass Dr., R.R. 1, Pender Island, V0N 2M0), or call the **Canadian Gulf Islands Reservation Service** (☎250-539-5390) for free accommodation and adventure-package bookings.

Galiano Island

The first thing you will notice upon arriving in

Galiano is the scarcity of infrastructure and commercial development. The inhabitants's passionate protests to protect the ecological balance have attracted worldwide attention. Their efforts have enabled Galiano to preserve its vast stretches of great natural landscapes. The island also has many meditation centres and retreats for New Age enthusiasts, such as **Serenity By-the-Sea** (*☎800-944-2655 or 250-539-2655*).

Galiano also features many bed and breakfasts and rustic cabins for rent as well as **campsites** in **Montague Harbour** (*☎250-539-2115*). There is also a good selection of restaurants here. **La Berengerie** (*☎250-539-5392*) is renowned for its Algerian food and lamb chops; it is also a bed and breakfast. Do not forget to bring bottled water as Galiano has no running water. Call **Galiano Getaways** (*☎250-539-5551 for B & B reservations*). They also offer adventure packages. For more information, call the **Galiano Island Chamber of Commerce** (*☎250-539-2233*).

Saturna Island

Saturna is perhaps the most isolated and least accessible of the Gulf Islands, and its inhabitants are determined to keep it that way. It has very limited facilities and only two restaurants. Nevertheless, there are many good reasons to visit the island. Nature lovers will be fascinated by its unusual fauna and flora, like the **giant mushrooms** at the base of **Mount Warburton**. On Canada Day (July 1st), a great annual lamb barbecue is organized. It is the largest local gathering of the year on the island. **Saturna Lodge** (*☎250-539-2254*) is one of the few inns here. Camping is forbidden on Saturna. For more information on accommodations, call ☎250-539-2930. To get to Saturna Island: **B.C. Ferries** (*☎888-223-3779 in BC, out of province: 250-386-3431*). Reservations are essential during the summer.

Outdoors

Located where the mountains meet the sea, a short distance from the wilds of British Columbia, Vancouver offers an extremely wide range of outdoor activities.

Downhill skiing, hiking in the woods, hang-gliding, salt-water swimming in the Strait of Georgia, sun-bathing on sandy beaches, sailboarding and surfing can all be enjoyed just a 30min or less from downtown.

The ski resorts of the Coast Mountains, north of Vancouver, are easily accessible by car via the Lions Gate Bridge. They boast substantial vertical drops (over 1000m), and offer a year-round cable car service to scenic lookouts on various mountaintops from which visitors can take in outstanding views of the city. To the south, the beaches flanking the central neighbourhoods mean that Vancouverites can go swim-ming in the ocean without leaving town – and the water isn't as polluted as you might think! Among the other popular activities, cycling and jogging in Stan-ley Park have become something of a ritual for many of the city's residents.

The local sports mania doesn't end there, however. Within the past few years, the city has built some impressive facilities for professional sports like football, hockey and most recently, basketball. This last sport, much more popular in the United States than in Canada, is indicative of the growing influence of American culture here in Vancouver.

For general information on all outdoor activities in the Greater Vancouver area, contact **Sport B.C.** *(509-1367 Broadway, Vancouver, V6H 4A9, ☎ 737-3000)* or the **Outdoor Recreation Council of B.C.** *(334-1367 Broadway, Vancouver, V6H 4A9, ☎ 737-3058)*. Both organizations offer many suggestions and information.

Vancouver Parks & Recreation
☎257-8400
The Vancouver Parks & Recreation provides all information on sports and recreation activities.

Altus Mountain Gear
137 West Broadway
☎876-5255
Everything for the mountains: waterproof gear, clothing, tents, backpacks...

Rental and some articles sold at cost.

Mountain Equipment Co-op
130 West Broadway
V5Y 1P3
between Manitoba St.
and Columbia St.
☎872-7858
Mountain Equipment Co-op is another excellent store specializing in outdoor gear and clothing.

Beaches

The Vancouver shoreline is made up in large part of easily accessible sandy beaches. All these beaches lie along English Bay where it is possible to walk, cycle, play volleyball and, of course, take a dip in the sea to fully enjoy the setting. Stanley Park is fringed by **Third Beach** and **Second Beach**, and then, further east, along Beach Avenue, by **First Beach** where hundreds of bathers brave the icy water to celebrate the New Year on January 1. A little farther east, **Sunset Beach** celebrates the day's end with gorgeous sunsets. At the southern edge of English Bay are **Kitsilano Beach**, **Jericho Beach**, **Locarno Beach**, **Spanish Banks Beach**, **Tower Beach** and, finally, **Wreck Beach** at the western edge of the University of

British Columbia campus.

Kitsilano Beach is enlivened by beach volleyball tournaments and by an assortment of sports facilities, including a basketball court. Locarno, Jericho and Spanish Banks beaches are quieter spots for family relaxation where walking and reading are key activities.

Outdoor Activities

Hiking

Stanley Park is definitely the best place go hiking in Vancouver with over 50km of trails through forest and greenery along the sea- and lakeshores, including the **Seawall**, an outstanding 8km trail flanked by giant trees.

If you like gardens and are heading through Chinatown, you won't need a pair of hiking boots to visit the **Dr. Sun Yat-Sen Classical Chinese Garden** (☎689-7133). Its little bridges and trails will guide you through a realm of peace and serenity (see "Exploring," p 70).

There are lots of places to go walking in the Point Grey area. Myriad trails crisscross the campus of the **University of British Columbia** (UBC). One of the best known runs across the famous **Endowment Lands, Pacific Spirit Park** which cover an area twice as large as Stanley Park. Others lead to the **UBC Botanical Gardens** *(summer $4.50; winter free; mid-Mar to mid-Oct, every day 10am to 6pm; winter, everyday 10am to 2:30pm; 6804 SW Marine Dr., ☎822-9666)*: the **Botanical**, **Alpine**, **Native**, **Physic**, **Food**, **Contemporary**, **Asian** and **Winter** gardens. They are all linked by well-marked paths, and the **Nitobe Memorial Garden** (see "Exploring," p 109). There is also a whole network of trails through the forest, and since UBC is located on a peninsula, all trails ultimately lead to the beach.

On the other side of Lions Gate Bridge, in North Vancouver, Capilano Road leads to **Capilano Park** (☎432-6350) where you'll find a trail offering sweeping views of the Capilano River. During summer, you can see the salmon swimming upriver.

Mountain hiking can be done on one of the peaks near the city centre. **Cypress Provincial Park** (☎924-2200), north of the municipality of West Vancouver, has sev-

Outdoors

eral hiking trails, among them the Howe Sound Crest Trail that leads to different mountains including The Lions and Mount Brunswick. The views over the west shore of Howe Sound are really quite spectacular. You must wear good shoes and bring food and water for these hikes. To get to Cypress Park by the Lions Gate Bridge, follow the signs west along the Trans-Canada Highway and take the Cypress Bowl Road exit. Take the time to stop at the lookout to contemplate Vancouver, the Strait of Georgia and, on a clear day, Mount Baker in the United States.

The hike up **Grouse Mountain** ★★★ (☎984-0661) is not particularly difficult, but the incline is as steep as 25° in places, so you have to be in good shape. It takes about 2hrs to cover the 3km trail which starts at the parking lot for the cable car. The view of the city from the top of the mountain is fantastic. If you are too tired to hike back down, take the cable car for the modest sum of $5.

Mount Seymour Provincial Park (☎986-2261) is another good hiking locale, offering two different views of the region. To the east is Indian Arm, a large arm of the sea extending into the valley.

A little further east in this marvellous mountain range on the north shore, magnificent **Lynn Headwaters Park** ★★★ is scored with forest trails. It is best known for its footbridge which stretches across an 80m deep gorge. Definitely not for the faint of heart! To get there, take Highway 1 from North Vancouver to the Lynn Valley Road exit and follow the signs, then turn right on Peters Road.

Lighthouse Park, in West Vancouver, is well suited to hiking on flatter terrain. From this site, you will be facing the University of British Columbia, the entrance to English Bay, and the Strait of Georgia. Take the Lions Gate Bridge and follow Marine Drive West, crossing the city of West Vancouver and hugging the seashore until you reach the western edge of English Bay. Turn left at Beacon Lane toward Lighthouse Park.

If you get off the 99 just after the affluent suburb of West Vancouver and head west to Horseshoe Bay, you'll come to lovely little **Whytecliff Park**, located on the seashore. Most people come here to go picnicking or scuba diving. For an interesting little excursion, follow the rocky trail out to **Whyte Island** at low tide. Before heading out to this big rock, make sure to check what time the tides are due to come in, or you'll end up with wet feet.

A 15min **ferry** *(BC Ferry, ☎250-386-3431)* ride from Horseshoe Bay transports you to **Bowen Island** ★★★ *(☎947-2216)* where hiking trails lead through a lush forest. Although you'll feel as if you're at the other end of the world, downtown Vancouver is only 5km away as the crow flies.

Cycling

The region has a multitude of trails for mountain biking. Just head to one of the mountains north of the city. A pleasant 8km ride runs along the Seawall in Stanley Park. Bicycle rentals are available at **Spokes Bicycle Rental** *(1798 West Georgia St., corner of Denman, ☎688-5141)*. Outside Vancouver, you can go cycling in the Fraser Valley, near farms or along secondary roads.

Heading away from Stanley Park on the **Seawall** that from English Bay, you'll reach another seawall, which is less crowded and better for cycling. About 15km long, it skirts **False Creek**, passes in front of the recently built housing complex on the grounds of the 1986 World Fair, invites cyclists to stop in at Science World, leads to the markets on Granville Island, and finally ends up back at the starting point on English Bay via the Burrard Bridge. More courageous visitors can follow the **Spanish Banks** beach all the way to UBC. You have to ride along roads during certain parts of the trip. To avoid getting lost, follow the green and white signs specifically posted for cyclists.

The 15min ferry ride from Horseshoe Bay out to little **Bowen Island** ★★★ *(☎947-2216)* is a worthwhile excursion. This perfectly lovely residential island has a network of quiet little country roads. You are likely to come across a deer or two, and make sure to keep an eye out for eagles soaring overhead. After a day of pedalling, you can enjoy a relaxing drink by the harbour at Snug Cove.

Bird-watching

Birders should make a trip to the **George C. Reifel Bird Sanctuary** ★★ *(5191 Robertson Road, Delta, ☎946-6980)* on Westham and Reifel islands. Dozens of species of migratory and non-migratory birds draw orthinology enthusiasts year-round to see aquatic birds, birds of prey, and many other varieties. Further south, several species can also be observed at Boundary Bay and Mud Bay as well as on Iona Island closer to Vancouver, next to the airport.

If you get off Highway 99 just after the affluent suburb of West Vancouver and head west to Horseshoe Bay, you'll come to lovely little **Whytecliff Park**, located on the seashore. Keep your ears tuned and your eyes peeled and you will probably spot some bald eagles in the tops of the tallest trees.

Bald Eagle

The largest bald eagle population in the world is found just 60km from Vancouver, in **Brackendale**, which lies alongside the 99 on the way to Whistler. Winter is a particularly good time to visit.

Eagle buffs mingle at the **Brackendale Art Gallery** *(Sat to Sun and statutory holidays, noon to 10pm; P.O. Box 100, Brackendale, V0N 1T0, ☎898-3333).*

Windsurfing

The pleasures afforded by the sea in Vancouver are definitely not to be taken lightly. **Howe Sound**, located alongside Highway 99 North on the way to Squamish, was slated to become a major harbour for giant freighters, but, to the great relief of local windsurfers, never did. The wind rushes into the hollow formed by the mountains on either side of the fjord, making this part of British Columbia a paradise for high-speed sailboarding. You can obtain all the necessary information about where to go at the **Squamish tourist office** *(37950 Cleveland Avenue, ☎892-9244).* To find out about wind conditions, call the **Windtalker Windline** *(☎926-9463).* A $10 fee covers insurance and potential rescue costs.

Sea Kayaking

Like the mountains, the water is a key part of life in Vancouver, and there is an almost unlimited number of ways to get out and enjoy the sea. One option is to tour the city by sea kayak. **False Creek** stretches all the way to Main Street and Science World, and you'll pass Granville Island along the way; by paddling around **Stanley Park**, you can reach Canada Place and the skyscrapers downtown. More courageous visitors can set out along **Indian Arm ★★★** to Deep Cove, an expedition likely to include a few encounters with seals and eagles. Kayak rentals are available at **Ecomarine Ocean Kayak Centre** *(1668 Duranleau Street, Granville Island, ☎689-7575)* on **Granville Island**.

Canoeing and Kayaking

Those who prefer running white water on smaller crafts can contact one of the following agencies that organize expeditions and will equip you from head to toe: **Whitewater Kayaking Association of B.C.** *(1367 Broadway, Vancouver, V6H 4A9, ☎222-1577)* or **Canadian Adventure Tours** *(Box 929, Whistler, V0N 1B0, ☎938-0727)* (a good place if you're passing through Whistler).

Canadian River Expeditions
301-3524 West 16th Ave.
Vancouver, V6R 3C1
☎**938-6651**
Canadian River Expeditions allows you to plan an expedition from Vancouver.

Sea To Sky Trails
105C-11831 80th Ave., Delta, V4C 7X6
☎**594-7701**
This small adventure travel agency is located in a suburb south of Vancouver.

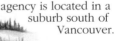

Rafting

Thrill-seekers will certainly appreciate the waterways around Vancouver. A white-water rafting paradise awaits visitors in the heart of Cascade Mountains, a semi-arid region less than 2hrs away from the city by car, on **Fraser River**, the greatest waterway in British Columbia in terms of flow.

descent is a real roller-coaster ride. Good luck!

Coquihalla River is another interesting and worthwhile destination. This powerful little river runs at the bottom of a deep canyon offering spectacular scenery. Another tumultuous little river, the **Nahatlatch**, is less frequented than its renowned counterparts, but worth considering nonetheless. The river closest to Vancouver on which to go rafting is the **Chilliwack**.

Certain parts of the river are sure to make your hair stand on end.

Thompson River (a tributary of Fraser River) is the best-known for white-river rafting. This beautiful emerald green river runs through a magnificent rocky, arid landscape. Experts will tell you the Thompson River

Despite its proximity to large urban centres, this river runs through a wild landscape. Over the course of the years, it has acquired a solid reputation among kayakers and canoeists.

Fraser River Raft Expeditions
Box 10, Yale, V0K 2S0
☎863-2336
Fraser River Raft Expeditions is located in the heart

of the Fraser River canyon and specializes in expeditions on the Fraser, Thompson, Coquihalla and Nahatlatch Rivers.

Hyak Wilderness Adventures
204B-1975 Maple St.
Vancouver, V6J 3S9
☎734-8622
This is a major rafting enterprise with an excellent reputation. It has the practical advantage of having its offices in Vancouver and offers expeditions on the Chilliwack, Fraser and Thompson Rivers.

REO Rafting Adventures
☎684-4438
REO Rafting Adventures is a big agency that organizes white-water rafting on the Chilliwack, Nahatlatch and Thompson Rivers. Group rates.

Sailing

Going for a sail is the best way to visit some of the lovely spots in **Vancouver Harbour**. Jericho Beach, in the Kitsilano area, is an excellent starting point. You can rent your own sailing dinghy or Hobie Cat at the **Jericho Sailing Centre Association** *(1300 Discovery Street,* **☎224-4177)**, or climb aboard a larger sailboat for a cruise of several hours or

several days. The **Cooper Boating Centre** *(1620 Duranleau Street, Granville Island,* **☎687-4110)** is a good place to keep in mind.

Pleasure Boating

Renting an outboard **motor boat** is as easy as renting a car. No special permit is required for you to putter around at your leisure or speed across the water, as long as you stay near the shore. You'll find everything you need at **Granville Island Boat Rentals** *(16296 Duranleau Street, Granville Island,* **☎682-6287)**.

Fishing

Salt-water Fishing

Vancouver is the starting point for unforgettable fishing. When it comes to sea fishing, **salmon** reigns supreme. Before casting your line, you must obtain a permit from a specialized outfitter from whom you can also rent out the necessary equipment. They have boats, know the best locations, supply equipment and often meals, too. Make sure you are dressed appropriately, though. Even when the sun is out, it can get very cold on the open sea. It is also essential that you not forget your fishing permit. You will find a mine of information in *BC Sportsfishing* magazine *(contact Rick Taylor, 909 Jackson Crescent, New Westminster, V3L 4S1, ☎683-4871, ≈683-4318)*.

Coho Sports

4152 Penticton St.
☎*435-7333*
≈*435-7333*

Coho Sports offers salmon fishing in such regions as the Sunshine Coast. Trips depart from Vancouver, last half a day to four days, and include meals. Coho Sports also provides apartments for those who opt for longer stays. All fishing gear is supplied.

Black Gold Lodge

summer only
3826 Azalea Pl., Port Coquitlam
☎*941-3228*

Black Gold Lodge offers not only accommodation but boat rentals and sea-fishing gear as well.

West Coast Fishing Resorts

Suite 190, 5400 Airport Rd. S.
Richmond, V7B 1B4
☎*278-3130 or 800-810-8933*
≈*278-3120*

West Coast Fishing Resorts is a large salmon fishing centre with three sea fishing camps at which you can stay: Whale Channel, Milbanke and Sound River

Inlet. Open from May to September.

Westin Bayshore Yacht Charters

1601 West Georgia St.
☎*691-6936*

Westin Bayshore Yacht Charters has an impressive fleet of fishing yachts.

Fresh-water Fishing

With an infinite number of lakes and rivers, trout fishing in British Columbia is always excellent. Permits are sold in all camping equipment stores as well as at **Ruddik's Fly Fishing** *(1654 Duranleau St., Granville Island, ☎681-3747)*, a good shop for this sport. Thousands of flies for catching every kind of fish in the area can be purchased here. The owner will gladly offer advice. Vancouver is the starting point to equip yourself and make inquiries, though you will have to leave the city to fish on a river or lake. The interior region and Cariboo Country are prime destinations for anglers in Vancouver. You can also purchase an issue of *BC Sportsfishing* at almost any newsagent's or call on fishing clubs or outfitters. A few good outfitters are listed below. Many of these are located outside Vancouver, though they do have booking offices in the city so as to be accessible to their clientele.

N.B. Salt-water and fresh-water fishing licenses are not interchangeable.

Pinantan Lake Family Resort
(3838 West 22nd Ave., Vancouver, V6S 1J7, ☎222-2698, ≈222-2698) is situated in Cariboo Country, 4hrs from Vancouver. As its name suggests, this establishment caters to families. Guests can spend the night in one of the charming little houses by the lake.

Sheridan Park Resort
Comp. #200, West Sheridan Site R.R. # 1, Lone Butte ,V0K 1X0
☎*(250) 593-4643*
www.sheridanlakeresort.com
Sheridan Park Resort is another organization that offers fresh-water fishing excursions.

Crazy Bear Lake Lodge
Box 34312, Vancouver, V6J 4P3
☎*739-0789*
≈*739-0789*
The Crazy Bear Lake Lodge is open from June to September. The owner speaks German, Spanish and English, of course. Pets are welcome and the fishing is excellent.

Taseko Lake Lodge
204-814 West 15th St.
North Vancouver, V7P 1M6
☎*988-7143*
≈*988-7092*
Open all year round, Taseko Lake Lodge offers equipped log cabins that each can accommodate up to 12 people; meals are included. Canoes are available, and a guide will take you to prime locations. Guests can also go horseback riding here.

Elkin Creek Guest Ranch
4462 Marion Rd.
North Vancouver, V7K 2V2
☎*984-4666*
≈*984-4686*
Situated in Cariboo Country, Elkin Creek Guest Ranch offers 23 rooms and lodgings, nine of which have running water, from April to October. The ranch can accommodate up to 40 guests. Boats, permits and equipment are provided. Since Elkin Creek is a ranch, guests can also enjoy horseback riding here.

For more information on fresh water fishing, you can visit the **Granville Island Sport Fishing Museum** (see p 100 in "Exploring").

Whale-watching

Visitors can admire great marine mammals on the outskirts of Vancouver, including **grey whales**, **killer whales** and other **finbacks**. There are observation boats on Vancouver Island. Here are a few places that can help you plan your outing:

Outdoors

Bluewater Adventures
☎980-3800 or 888-877-1770
For multi-day excursions

Seaker Adventure Tours
☎800-728-0244

Stubbs Island Whale Watching
Box 7, Dept. BCOA, Telegraph Cove
V0N 3J0
☎250-928-3185 or 800-665-3066
Stubbs Island Whale Watching specializes in the observation of killer whales. A hydrophone records the singing of whales, and you can even keep the cassette.

Mountaineering

A trip to Vancouver without tackling the snow-covered peaks that surround the city would be a real shame. The **Federation of Mountain Clubs of B.C.** (336-1367 Broadway, Vancouver, V6H 4A9, ☎737-3053) is a very reliable club with experienced instructors. Excursions are organized on a regular basis.

Rock-climbing

As you are aware, Vancouver is surrounded by mountains. On that account, rock-climbing sites are hardly lacking. One of the best known in western North America, **Squamish Chief**, lies 60km from Vancouver. This rock, at an altitude of 780m, is considered the second largest monolith in the world, after El Capitan in California. Squamish Chief boasts rock climbing routes: you have only to hook your karabiners.

Mescalito Adventure Company (50639 O'Byrne, Chilliwack, ☎858-2300) will assist you in climbing the cliffs and mountains overlooking the Fraser Valley.

Helicopter Sightseeing

If Vancouver's scenery has already won you over, here is something that will truly take your breath away! A glacier-skimming helicopter ride over snow-covered peaks and turquoise lakes is a must. Some agencies even offer landings on the gla-

Vancouver's skyline offers an imposing background to the sailboats drifting in its port.
- C. Moreno

Sunset over Vancouver, a prosperous, modern city.
Walter Bibikow

In winter, Vancouver's majestic mountains turn into a paradise for snow-lovers. - *Sean O'Neill*

ciers. Though somewhat pricey, you will have unforgettable memories and extraordinary photographs too.

Mountain Heli Sports
4340 Sundial Crescent
Whistler
☎932-2070
Mountain Heli Sports is a very versatile agency, offering not only flights over mountains and Vancouver, but heli-skiing as well.

Harbour City Helicopters
104-5225 216th St.
Langley, B.C., V3A 4R1
☎534-7918
⇒532-3946
This agency is located in the Vancouver suburbs at the gateway to the Fraser Valley.

Whistler Heli-Ski
Box 849, Whistler, V0N 1B0
☎932-7007 or 888-Heli-Ski
Whistler Heli-Ski is a very well-known agency in Whistler for heli-skiing.

Valley Helicopters
63235 Flood-Hope Rd., R.R. 2
Hope, V0X 1L0
☎869-2131
At the gateway to the city of Hope, a stone's throw from Trans-Canada Highway 1, Valley Helicopters will take you flying over Mount Baker and Manning Provincial Park.

Vancouver Helicopters
5455D Airport Rd. S.
Richmond
☎270-1484 or 800-987-4354
Vancouver Helicopters is located right near Vancouver International Airport. This enterprise has a fine reputation and will take you anywhere you want.

Kite Flying

With its 26km of beaches, Vancouver is the perfect place to go fly a kite. The most renowned spot for this activity is **Vanier Park**, which borders the beaches on English Bay, behind the Vancouver Museum. To get there, take the Burrard Bridge out of the downtown area and follow Chestnut Street through the pretty neighbourhood of Kitsilano. If you need equipment, **Kite Horizon Aerosports** *(1807 Burrard Street,* **☎738-5867)** has an infinite array of kites, including some high-performance models.

Horseback Riding

Horseback riding opportunities are virtually limitless around Vancouver, with

Outdoors

many bridle paths along forest roads. Contact **Back Country Horsemen of B.C.** *(Fraser Valley, ☎856-8276; Mission ☎462-0464)*, which has representatives throughout British Columbia, or write to the provincial head office *(SS1, Site 5, Box 70, Cranbrook, V1C 6H3)*. Keep in mind that this is a private club.

In-line Skating

In-line skating, more commonly known as rollerblading, is a standard summer activity in Vancouver. Although you'll see skaters all over, the most popular place to go is around Stanley Park on the **Seawall**, a fantastic eight-kilometre trail flanked by a century-old forest. Skate rentals are available at many places along the beach, including **Outa-Lines Inlines** *(1251 Pacific Boulevard, ☎899-2257)*.

Golf

Vancouver is unquestionably the golf capital of western Canada with golf for all tastes and budgets. Golf courses in Vancouver

and its surrounding areas are virtually all hilly and offer spectacular views of the ocean and especially the mountains which loom over all parts of the region. It should be noted that all golf clubs require appropriate attire. For lack of space, there are very few courses in Vancouver itself, but the suburbs boast one at practically every turn.

University Golf Club
5185 University Blvd.
☎224-1818
The University Golf Club is one of the best-known in town and among the priciest. It is situated a stone's throw from the University of British Columbia (UBC). Sean Connery has played here.

Peace Portal Golf Course
16900 Fourth Avenue, Surrey
☎538-4818
The oldest public golf course, the Peace Portal Golf Course was founded in 1928 and is open year-round. It lies along Highway 99, near the U.S. border, in the suburb of Surrey.

Mayfair Lakes Golf and Country Club
5460 No. 7 Road, Richmond
☎273-6521
In Richmond, another of the city's southern suburbs, the Mayfair Lakes Golf and Country Club has a top-notch green surrounded by water.

Furry Creek
Britannia Beach, BC, V0N 1J0
☎*922-9576 or 922-9461*
No golf course boasts a more spectacular setting than Furry Creek, located just past the village of Lions Bay, on **Howe Sound**, which Highway 99 North runs alongside on its way to Squamish. Nestled away in a splendid landscape, this course is more than just pleasant; imagine the sea stretched out beside towering, snow-capped peaks. Amazing.

Fraserview Golf Course
7800 Vivian Dr.
☎*327-5616*
The Fraserview Golf Course is an affordable golf course, managed by the city (Vancouver Board of Parks and Recreation Public Course) and located at the southern tip of Vancouver.

Langara Golf Course
6706 Alberta St.
☎*257-8355*
The Langara Golf Course is also a municipal golf course (Vancouver Board of Parks and Recreation Public Course), situated southeast of town.

Gleneagles
6190 Marine Dr., West Vancouver
☎*921-7353*
Right near the lovely village of Horseshoe Bay and 15min from Vancouver, is a very inexpensive golf course that is sometimes

jam-packed on weekends, but the scenery makes playing here worth the wait.

Seymour Golf and Country Club
3723 Mt. Seymour Pkwy
North Vancouver
☎*929-2611*
In North Vancouver, in a very mountainous region, is the Seymour Golf and Country Club. Oddly enough, this club is only open to the public Mondays through Fridays.

Burnaby Mountain Golf Club
7600 Halifax, Burnaby
☎*280-7355*
The Burnaby Mountain Golf Club is located in a lovely setting, close to Simon Fraser University (SFU), 15min east of Vancouver.

Riverway Golf Course
9001 Riverway Pl., Burnaby
☎*280-4653*
The Riverway Golf Course is another beautiful golf course in Burnaby.

**Westwood Plateau
Golf & Country Club**
3251 Plateau Blvd., Coquitlam
☎*552-0777*
In Coquitlam, a suburb northeast of Vancouver, is the Westwood Plateau Golf & Country Club, a brand new golf course with spectacular scenery and grounds. Be advised, however, that the golf marshal is not overly fond of slow players and, considering the $95 admission fee, you had

Outdoors

best be a fine player!

Whistler Golf Clubs

Whistler golf courses have an excellent reputation, but playing here is hardly a bargain. These courses, of course, are closed throughout the winter because of snow. This is not the case for those in Vancouver and its suburbs, which are accessible all year long. Those keen enough to drive 2hrs out of Vancouver can check out the following places.

Nicklaus North Golf Club
Whistler
☎*938-9898*
The course at the Nicklaus North Golf Club course was designed by none other than the famous golf champion, Jack Nicklaus.

Chateau Whistler Golf Club
4612 Blackcomb Way, Whistler
☎*938-2090*
The Chateau Whistler Golf Club is part of the Canadian Pacific holiday resort complex. The ultimate in luxury!

Whistler Golf Club
4010 Whistler Way
☎*932-5538*
The Whistler Golf Club is a little less expensive than the Chateau club.

Driving Ranges in Vancouver and Surrounding Areas

University Golf Club
5185 University Boulevard
☎*224-1818*

Musqueam Golf Club
3904 West 51st Avenue
☎*266-2334.*
An executive 18 hole course, par 60.

Seymour Golf and Country Club
3723 Mt. Seymour Parkway
North Vancouver
☎*929-2611*

Riverway Golf Course
9001 Riverway Place, Burnaby
☎*280-4653*

**Westwood Plateau
Golf & Country Club**
3251 Plateau Boulevard, Coquitlam
☎*552-0777*

Mayfair Lakes Golf Course
5460 No. 7 Road, Richmond
☎*276-0505*

Pitch & Putt

Pitch & Putt is a simplified version of golf. Although the rules are quite similar, you don't necessarily have to be a practiced golfer to play.

For about $12 per person (equipment included), you can spend a pleasant day with your friends or family outside amidst flowers and impeccable greenery. Vancouver has three Pitch & Putt courses, the best known being the one in **Stanley Park** *(c/o Parks Office, 2099 Beach Avenue, ☎257-8400)*. The other two are in **Queen Elizabeth Park** *(☎874-8336)*, which stretches south of town, and **Rupert Park** *(3402 Charles St., ☎257-8364)*, to the east.

Health Clubs

If you are a member of a gym in your own country or home town, **your card could be accepted in Vancouver**. Many clubs, in fact, are part of international organizations. Check whether your card is valid by contacting your club or those in Vancouver. Those listed below are all located in the Vancouver area.

Bentall Centre Athletic Club
Bentall 4, 1055 Dunsmuir St.
☎**689-4424**
The Bentall Centre Athletic Club is a typical business club, located in the business district.

Denman Fitness Company
1731 Comox St.
☎**688-2484**
Denman Fitness Company is a small and very pleasant neighbourhood sports club with many gay members.

Fitness Quest Gym
444 West Sixth Ave.
☎**879-7855**
The Fitness Quest Gym is a well-equipped independent club.

Fitness World
1214 Howe St.
☎**681-3232**
Fitness World is part of the biggest chain of health clubs in Vancouver.

Fitness World
1989 Marine Dr., North Vancouver
☎**986-3487**
This centre is the largest and poshest link in the Fitness World chain. An absolute must. Easy parking.

Fitness World
555 West 12th Ave.
☎**876-1009**
Here is another Fitness World. This one is ultra-high-tech and sometimes jam-packed at the end of the day.

Olympic Athletic Club
212 First St. W., Vancouver
☎**708-9441**
Far to the west of the city, this club has an excellent reputation.

Outdoors

RZ Lady Sport
1681 Chestnut
☎*737-4355*
As its name suggests, RZ
Lady Sport caters only to
women.

RZ Sports Club
200-1807 West First Ave.
☎*737-4355*
Situated a stone's throw
from RZ Lady Sport, this
gym is mixed.

Cross-country Skiing

Less than a 30min from
Vancouver, three ski resorts
welcome snow-lovers from
morning to evening. In
**Cypress Provincial Park, on
Hollyburn Ridge ★**, Cypress
Bowl Ski Areas *(☎926-5612)*
offers 25 kilometres of
mechanically maintained
trails suitable for all catego-
ries of skiers. These trails
are frequented day and
evening by cross-country
skiers. There are also trails
at **Grouse Mountain**
(☎984-0661) and **Mount
Seymour Provincial Park**
(☎986-2261).

Downhill Skiing

What makes Vancouver a
truly magical place is the
combination of sea and
mountains. The cold season
is no exception as residents
desert the beaches and seaside paths to crowd the ski
hills which are literally sus-
pended over the city. There
are four ski resorts close to
the city: **Mount Seymour**
*(adults $26; 1700 Mount Sey-
mour Rd., North Vancouver,
B.C., V7G 1L3; Upper Level
Hwy. heading east, Deep Cove
Exit, information ☎986-2261,
ski conditions ☎718-7771,
☎/≈986-2267)*, a family resort with beginner trails,
situated east of North Vancouver, above Deep Cove;
Grouse Mountain *(adults $28,
night skiing $20; 6400 Nancy
Greene Way, North Vancou-
ver, information ☎984-0661,
ski conditions ☎986-6262, ski
school ☎980-9311)*, a small
resort accessible by cable
car, which offers an
unobstructed view of Van-
couver that is as magnificent by day as it is by night;
Cypress Bowl *(adults $35,
night skiing $23; from North
Vancouver, take TransCanada
Highway 1, heading west for
16km, then follow road signs.
Information and ski conditions ☎926-5612)*, a resort
for the most avid skiers,
also offers magnificent
views of Howe Sound and
of the city. For more affordable skiing, try the vil-
lage-style **Hemlock Valley
Resort** *(adults $32, night ski-
ing $11; Hwy. 1 heading east,
Agassizou Harrisson Hot
Springs Exit; information
☎797-4411, ski conditions*

☎ *520-6222, ☏ 797-4440, accommodation reservations* ☎ *797-4444).* Situated at the eastern tip of Vancouver's urban area, in the heart of the Cascade Mountains, this resort boasts an abundance of snow and a spectacular view of Mount Baker in the United States. As soon as enough snow blankets the slopes, in late November or early December, these four ski resorts are open every day until late at night thanks to powerful neon lighting. It should be noted, however, that the first three resorts do not provide accommodation (consult Tour F: Burrard Inlet in the "Accommodations" chapter, p 137 for the nearest hotels).

Those who prefer skiing outside the metropolitan area can head to **Whistler**. This ski resort is considered the best in North America, with an annual snowfall of 9m and a 1,600m vertical drop. There are two mountains to choose from: **Whistler Mountain** and **Blackcomb Mountain** (*hotel reservations,* ☎ *604-932-4222; from Vancouver,* ☎ *685-3650; from the US,* ☎ *800-634-9622).* The skiing here is extraordinary, and the facilities ultramodern – but mind your budget! You will understand why prices are so high upon seeing hordes of Japanese and American tourists monopo-

lize the hotels and intermediate ski runs. Whistler and Blackcomb Mountains together make up the largest skiing area in Canada. These world-class, twin ski playgrounds are blessed with heavy snowfalls and boast enough hotels to house a city's entire population. This top-of-the-range ski metropolis also offers the possibility of gliding through pristine powder and, weather permitting, you will find yourself swooshing through an incredibly beautiful alpine landscape.

Whistler Mountain (*adults $42; from Vancouver, Hwy. 99 heading north for 130 km, information* ☎ *932-3434 or 800-766-0449, ski conditions* ☎ *932-4191)* is the elder of the two resorts. Experts, powderhounds and skijumpers will all flock to Peak Chair, the chair lift that leads to the top of Whistler Mountain. From its summit, diehard skiers and snowboarders have access to a ski area composed of blue (intermediate) and

Outdoors

expert (black-diamond and double-diamond) trails, covered in deep fleecy snow. **Blackcomb Mountain** *(adults $59; in Whistler; from Vancouver, Hwy. 99 heading north for 130 km; 4545 Blackcomb Way, Whistler, B.C., V0N 1B4; information ☎932-3141 or 800-766-0449, ski conditions ☎932-4211)* is the "stalwart" skiing Mecca of ski buffs in North America.

For years now, a fierce debate has been waged by skiers over which of the two mountains (Whistler or Blackcomb) is the best. One thing is certain, Blackcomb wins first place for its vertical drop of 1,609m. Check out the glacier at Blackcomb – it is truly magnificent!

N.B.: Snowboarding is permitted at all of these resorts.

Accommodations

V ancouver is a big city with lodgings for all tastes and budgets.

A ll accommodations shown here are well located, within walking distance of bus stops and, in most cases, in or near the downtown area. **Super Natural British Columbia** *(☎800-663-6000)* can make reservations for you.

Ulysses's Favourites

For the romantic atmosphere:
Hotel Vancouver, p 140
Wedgewood Hotel, p 140
Sheraton Wall
    Centre Hotel, p 143
Terminal City Club, p 139

For the pool:
Westin Bayshore, p 145

For the lobby:
Pan Pacific Hotel, p 140

For the view:
Landmark Hotel, p 144
Sylvia Hotel, p 142
Carmana Plaza, p 143
Plaza 500 Hotel, p 150
Vancouver Suites
    By the Sea, p 142

Tour A: Gastown

The Dominion Hotel
$50 bkfst incl
sb/pb, tv, ℜ
210 Abbott St.
☎*681-6666*
⚏*681-5855*
Located in the heart of Gastown, the rooms at The Dominion Hotel have re-

cently been renovated. Three blocks from the stadium and the Convention Centre, and not far from Chinatown, downtown and Stanley Park.

Tour B: Chinatown and East Vancouver

Simon Fraser University
$48
sb, K, ℝ, P
Room 212
McTaggart-Cowan Hall, Burnaby
☎*291-4503*
⇌*291-5598*
This student residence is available from May to August and is located atop a mountain. If you bring a sleeping bag, a room for two costs about $40, saving you about $10. SFU is 20 kilometres east of downtown Vancouver.

Tour C: Downtown

Vancouver Downtown YHA
$19 members
$23 non-members
1114 Burnaby St.
V6E 1P1
☎*684-4565*
⇌*684-4540*
Vancouver Downtown YHA is a big hostel (239 beds) right downtown at the corner of Thurlow. Common kitchen and tv room; coin-laundry.

YMCA
$39
sb, tv, K, ≈
955 Burrard St.
☎*681-0221*
⇌*681-1630*
This establishment on the corner of Nelson Street is not actually restricted to men; families are also welcome. The building is brand-new and offers rooms accommodating from one to five people.

Travelodge Vancouver Centre
$79
tv, ℜ, P
1304 Howe St.
☎*682-2767*
⇌*682-6225*
The Travelodge Vancouver Centre offers a discount to seniors and groups. Relax in the heated outdoor pool before dining at its restaurant.

Best Western Downtown Vancouver
$89
tv
718 Drake St.
corner Granville St.
☎*669-9888*
⇌*669-3440*
Facing Granville Street, this brand-new, comfortable hotel is situated near interesting attractions. If you don't have a car, there's a bus stop just before the entrance to the Granville Bridge.

Ramada Vancouver Centre
$90
tv
898 West Broadway
☎*872-8661*
≈*872-2270*
Located in the eastern part of Vancouver, this hotel belongs to the Ramada hotel chain which specializes in accommodations for large groups and families. Comfortable rooms and impeccable, personalized service.

Sandman Hotel
$100
tv
180 West Georgia St.
☎*681-2211*
≈*681-8009*
Situated near theatres and downtown, the Sandman Hotel has 216 comfortable rooms. The Shark Club Bar & Grill (see p 177) is the hotel restaurant.

Hampton Inn & Suites
$109 bkfst incl
tv, ◷, ≡
111 Robson St.
☎*602-1008*
≈*602-1007*
The rooms at the Hampton Inn & Suites are spacious and cosy. Only a stone's throw away from the major theatres and the new library.

Bosman's Motor Hotel
$139
≡, ≈, P
1060 Howe St.
☎*682-3171*
☎*888-BOSMANS*
≈*684-4010*
Bosman's Motor Hotel is in the heart of the city, close to the National Museum, theatres and beaches. The rooms are spacious and modern.

Terminal City Club
$160
tv, ℜ
837 West Hastings St.
☎*681-4121*
≈*681-9634*
The favourite place for business travellers, this luxurious establishment has an elegant style. It has 60 cosy rooms with a cheerful decor. Its poolroom, golf simulator, ocean view and attentive service will make your stay memorable.

Canadian Pacific Waterfront Centre Hotel
$220-$350
tv, ≈, ◷, ✖, ≡, △, ⊛, P, ℜ, ♿
900 Canada Place Way
☎*691-1991*
☎*800-441-1414*
≈*691-1999*
The Canadian Pacific Waterfront Centre Hotel is a luxury hotel located just a few steps from Gastown. It has 489 rooms.

Wedgewood Hotel

$240

☺, △, ≡, ℜ

845 Hornby St., V6Z 1V2

☎**689-7777**

☎**800-663-0666**

⇄**668-3074**

The Wedgewood Hotel is small enough to have retained some character and style. In particular, It features a lovely lobby complete with shiny brass accents, cosy fireplace and distinguished art, and is large enough to offer a certain measure of privacy and professionalism. This is a popular option for business trips and romantic weekend getaways.

Hotel Vancouver

$340

tv, ≈, ⊛, ☺, △, ℜ, ℝ, ✕, ৬, P

900 West Georgia St.

☎**684-3131**

☎**800-441-1414**

⇄**662-1929**

The Hotel Vancouver belongs to the Canadian Pacific Hotel chain. It was built in the 1930s in the château-style characteristic of Canadian railway hotels, of which the Château Frontenac in Québec City was a precursor. In 1939 it hosted George VI, the first British monarch to visit Canada. You will find tranquillity and luxury in the heart of downtown near Robson Street and Burrard Street. The hotel has 508 rooms.

Metropolitan Hotel

$365

☺, ⊛, ≡, ✕, ৬, tv, ℜ, △, ≈, P

645 Howe St.

☎**687-1122 or 800-667-2300**

⇄**689-7044**

Once a Delta hotel, the Metropolitan Hotel is located right downtown, just steps from the business district. These luxury accommodations also have a luxurious price tag. Diva, the hotel's restaurant with its pleasant staff and a cosy ambience, is worth trying.

Pan Pacific Hotel Vancouver

$410

≡, ⊛, ☺, tv, ≈, △, P, ℜ, ৬, ✕

300-999 Canada Place

☎**662-8111**

in Canada:

☎**800-663-1515**

in the US:

☎**800-937-1515**

⇄**685-8690**

The luxurious Pan Pacific Hotel Vancouver is located in Canada Place, on the shore of Burrard Inlet facing North Vancouver, with a good view of port activities. The hotel has 506 rooms and a magnificent lobby with its marble decor, 20m-high ceilings and panoramic view of the ocean.

Tour D: The West End

Barclay Hotel
$75 bkfst incl.
tv, ℜ
1348 Robson St.
☎**688-8850**
≈**688-2534**
The Barclay Hotel is an older though spotless establishment with direct access to a pricey restaurant.

Buchan Hotel
$75 sb, $100 pb
children under 12 free
bicycle and ski racks, tv
1906 Haro Street
☎**685-5354 or 800-668-6654**
≈**685-5367**
Buchan Hotel is located in the West End residential area near Stanley Park beneath the trees. At the end of Haro Street, on Lagoon Drive, three municipal tennis courts are accessible to guests. Other tennis courts, a golf course and hiking trails can be found near this 61-room, three-storey hotel. Smoking on the premises is prohibited.

Burrard Motor Inn
$79
pb, tv, K
1100 Burrard St.
in front of St. Paul's Hospital
☎**681-2331**
≈**681-9753**
The Burrard Motor Inn is located near Robson, the lively street in the West End which has restaurants, cinemas and shops. Some rooms have kitchenettes. Free indoor parking.

Greenbrier Apartment Motor Hotel
$79 to $189
tv, K, ℜ
1393 Robson St.
☎**683-4558**
≈**669-3109**
The Greenbrier Apartment Motor Hotel is particularly popular with globetrotters. You'll meet world travellers who have decided to take a break in Vancouver. Weekly and monthly rates.

Executive Accommodations
$800/week
tv, K
☎**800-557-8483**
"Like home" is the motto of the Executive Accommodations chain, which offers apartments and completely furnished homes, including daily cleaning service.

Rosellen Suites
$100
tv, K
2030 Barclay St.
☎**689-4807**
≈**684-3327**
Located in the heart of the West End near Stanley Park and downtown, these completely furnished suites have one or two bedrooms, kitchenettes and all the modern conveniences. They can be rented on a short- or long-term basis. Cost varies slightly depending upon the length of stay.

Sylvia Hotel
$115
tv, K, ℜ, 🐾, P
1154 Gilford Street
☎*681-9321*

Located just a few steps from English Bay, this charming old hotel, built in the early 1900s, offers unspoiled views and has 118 simple rooms. People come for the atmosphere, but also for food and drink at the end of the day. For those on lower budgets, rooms without views are offered at lower rates. The manager of this ivy-covered hotel is a Frenchman who is fully and justifiably dedicated to his establishment. Request a southwest-facing room (one facing English Bay) in order to benefit from magical sunsets over the bay.

Vancouver's Suites By the Sea
$130
pb, tv, K, ☺
The Meridien at 910 Beach
☎*609-5100*
⇄*609-5111*

Small apartments or suites with one to three bedrooms with a magnificent view of the sea. Kitchen, washing machines, offices for business meetings and an exercise room. Prices vary according to the length of stay. Many interesting attractions nearby.

Tropicana Motor Inn
$139
tv, K, ℜ, △, ≈
1361 Robson St.
☎*687-6631*
⇄*687-5724*

The affordable Tropicana Motor Inn rarely has the "no vacancy" sign up. A great location right in the action on the busy part of Robson probably has something to do with it. It is not a palace, but is perfect for younger travellers and people on a tighter budget.

Riviera Motor Inn
$148
tv, K
1431 Robson St.
☎*685-1301*
⇄*685-1335*

The comfortable and simple luxuriousness of the Riviera Motor Inn is nevertheless a bit expensive.

Robsonstrasse City Motor Inn
$149
tv, K
1394 Robson St.
☎*687-1674 or 888-667-8877*
⇄*685-7808*

The Robsonstrasse City Motor Inn is another affordable Robson Street option. The clientele is similar to that of the Tropicana (see above).

Oceanside
$150/day, $700 per week
$1,500 per month
pb, tv, P
1847 Pendrell St.
☎*682-5641*
Complete apartments, with separate bedrooms; right downtown, a walk away from the major attractions.

 West End Guest House Bed & Breakfast
$150 bkfst incl.
P, ⊗
no children under 12
1362 Haro St.
☎*681-2889*
⇌*688-8812*
www.westendguesthouse.com
This magnificent inn set in a turn-of-the-century Victorian house is well situated near a park and Robson Street. Evan Penner is your host. A minimum two-day stay may apply. The West End Guest House has an excellent reputation. (Nearby, at 1415 Barclay St., is Roedde House, built in Victorian-Edwardian style in 1893 and designed by none other than the architect Francis Rattenbury, who also created the Vancouver Art Gallery, the legislature building in Victoria and the Empress Hotel.)

 Carmana Plaza
$160
tv, K, ⊘
1128 Alberni St.
☎*683-1399*
⇌*683-1391*
The Carmana Plaza is a luxurious, all-suite facility. Each suite has a view of the sea or city. Enjoy its numerous amenities, including a kitchen, office and conference rooms for business travellers, exercise room, cleaning service, security guard and parking.

Blue Horizon Hotel
$170
tv, ℜ, △, ≈, ≡, ⊛, ⊘, ᴖ
1225 Robson St.
☎*688-1411 or 800-663-1333*
⇌*688-4461*
The Blue Horizon Hotel recently re-opened after extensive renovations. Each of the 214 rooms affords an exceptional view of the city. Reasonably priced meals are served in the interior "granite" decor or out on the terrace facing Robson Street.

 Sheraton Wall Centre Hotel
$160
tv, ℜ, ⊘, P
1088 Burrard St.
☎*331-1000*
⇌*893-7123*
This hotel has remarkable architecture, a creatively decorated interior, a colourful bar, restaurants with

innovative cuisine, a distinguished ambience, a welcoming garden and a sports club.

Chez Phillipe
$175-$225 bkfst incl.
tv, K, P
by appointment only
☎*649-2817*

Chez Phillipe is located in the heart of Vancouver in the West End neighbourhood, two steps away from False Creek in a very holiday-like setting. It's a luxurious apartment on the 17th floor of a modern highrise built at the entrance to the Seawall.To get to Granville Island Market, you have to take a charming little ferry that leaves from the foot of the building and crosses False Creek. A generous breakfast is included in the price and you can even cook for yourself if you like. Guests also have access to a dishwasher, a washing machine and a dryer as well as a full bathroom with a separate shower and a terrace. By reservation only.

Parkhill Hotel
$189
tv, ☉, ℜ, △, ≈
1160 Davie St.
☎*685-1311 or 800-663-1525*
⇰*681-0208*

The Parkhill Hotel is right in the middle of Vancouver's gay village. The rooms are perfectly comfortable and the restaurant serves

fine Japanese cuisine. Just steps from English Bay and Stanley Park.

Landmark Hotel
$200
tv, ⊛, ☉, ℜ, △, ≈, ᕻ
1400 Robson St.
☎*687-0511*
☎*800-830-6144*
⇰*687-2801*

The Landmark Hotel truly is a landmark with it 40 floors and its revolving resto-bar at the top. The view is fascinating and quite an experience!

Listel O'Doul's Hotel
$200
tv, ℜ, △, ⊛, ᕻ
1300 Robson St.
☎*684-8461*
☎*800-663-5491*
⇰*684-8326*

The Listel O'Doul's Hotel on Robson also houses a friendly, though slightly noisy, pub and a good restaurant. The service and comfort are indisputable.

Pacific Palisades Hotel
$225-$290
tv, ≈, P, ℜ, ℝ, K, ᕻ, ☉
1277 Robson Street
☎*688-0461 or 800-663-1815*
⇰*688-4374*

Pacific Palisades Hotel is part of the Shangri-La hotel chain. Its two towers, totalling 233 rooms, offer superb views of the sea and the mountains. Rooms facing north on the upper floors provide especially fine mountain views. A big pool and a well-equipped gymnasium are available to guests. All services for tourists or business travellers are looked after with professionalism. The staff is friendly and efficient.

Coast Plaza at Stanley Park
$250-$330
≈, △, *tv*, ☺, ℜ, *K*, ℝ, ✻, ⅋, *P*
1763 Comox St.
☎*688-7711*
☎*800-663-1144*
⇍*688-5934*
If you are looking for a big, modern, American-style hotel close to the beach, this 267-room establishment is a good choice. The restaurant serves everything, and the food is decent.

Sutton Place Hotel
$265-$415
⊛, ☺, ≈, △, ℝ, ℜ, ⅋
845 Burrard St.
☎*682-5511*
☎*800-961-7555*
⇍*682-5513*
The Sutton Place Hotel, formerly the Meridien, offers 397 rooms and the full range of five-star services normally provided by the top hotel chains. The European decor has been maintained. If you are a chocolate lover, don't miss the chocolate buffet served on Fridays.

Apricot Cat Guest House
$95-$115 bkfst incl.
pb, tv
628 Union St.
☎*215-9898*
⇍*255-9271*
The Apricot Cat Guest House is a beautiful, old restored house that is just at the outer edge of downtown not far from Stanley Park, the conference centre, GM Place and Gastown. It's well suited to business people for whom they have set up fax machines, guest-telephone lines and desks in larger rooms. The atmosphere is cozy, the rooms are bright and airy, and you can have your meals on the terrace with a view of the garden.

Westin Bayshore
$200-$300
tv, ℜ, △, ≈, *P*
1601 West Georgia St.
☎*682-3377*
⇍*687-3102*
The Westin Bayshore is a very classy place. Its setting is typically "Vancouver" with the surrounding mountains, the proximity of the sea and the city so close by. The 517 rooms each have their own charm, not to mention the stunning views. Staying here is like staying at a tropical resort.

Tour F: Burrard Inlet

The Globetrotter's Inn
$18 sb
45$ pb
tv
170 West Esplanade
North Vancouver
☎*988-2082*
⇌*987-8389*
The Globetrotter's Inn, in the heart of North Vancouver near the Seabus and the shops of Marine Drive and the Quay Market, is very affordable. Hostel-style dorm rooms are also available!

Capilano Bed & Breakfast
$60-$175 bkfst incl.
tv
1374 Plateau Dr.
☎*990-8889*
☎*877-990-8889*
⇌*990-5177*
The Capilano Bed & Breakfast is located close to Lions Gate Bridge. Skiers can easily get to Cypress Bowl (15min) and Grouse Mountain (8min). Except during rush hour, the hotel is 5min from Stanley Park, 10min from downtown and Chinatown, and about 25min from the airport. The rooms are attractive with some having nice views. The complete breakfasts are delicious. Prices for weekly stays can be negotiated and they offer a 20% discount on ski tickets for Grouse Mountain.

Horseshoe Bay Motel
$75
tv
6588 Royal Avenue, West Vancouver
☎*921-7454*
⇌*921-7464*
The Horseshoe Bay Motel, in the chic neighbourhood of West Vancouver, is advantageously located near the charming little town of Horseshoe Bay and the dock for the ferry to Nanaimo on Vancouver Island.

Canyon Court Motel
$110
tv, ≡, ≈
1748 Capilano Rd., North Vancouver
☎/⇌*988-3181*
The Canyon Court Motel is located right next to the Capilano Suspension Bridge, the Lions Gate Bridge and the Trans-Canada Highway. It is very comfortable and not too expensive.

Grouse Inn
$105
pb, ≡, ≈, tv
1633 Capilano Rd., North Vancouver
☎*988-7101 or 800-779-7888*
⇌*988-7102*
The Grouse Inn, located close to the Grouse Mountain cable car, is great for those who like to be near the mountains.

Accommodations

Summit View
$110-$150 bkfst incl.
tv, P, ℜ
5501 Cliffridge Pl.
☎990-1089
≈987-7167
To get here from the Lions
Gate Bridge, head toward
North Vancouver, turn right
on Marine Drive. Then, at
the first intersection, turn
left on Capilano Road, right
on Prospect Road, left on
Cliffridge Avenue and fi-
nally left on Cliffridge Place.
To get here from the Sec-
ond Narrows Bridge, take
Highway 1 west and exit
onto Capilano Road, then
continue as above.

Each room has its own
character. In the elegant
dining room, breakfast and
dinner are prepared according to your tastes or diet.
Rock-climbing, skiing, fishing, canoeing, swimming
and tennis are all possible
nearby. The management
offers bicycles to help you
discover the wonders of the
area. Low-season rates are
considerably less expensive
here.

Lonsdale Quay Hotel
$115-$175
tv, ≡, ⊛, ⊙, ℜ
123 Carrie Cates Court
North Vancouver
☎986-6111 or 800-836-6111
≈986-8782
The Lonsdale Quay Hotel is
a luxury hotel set magnifi-
cently near the shores of
Burrard Inlet, above the

huge covered Quay Market.
The rooms enjoy extraordi-
nary views of downtown
Vancouver.

Palms Guest House
$160-$239 bkfst incl.
pb, tv
3042 Marine Dr.
☎926-1159 or 800-691-4455
≈926-1451
To get here from Lions Gate
Bridge, go left to West Vancouver. Luxurious rooms
with a view of the ocean.
Easy access to Cypress
Bowl and Grouse Mountain
ski resorts. Close to the
charming little port of
Horseshoe Bay, ferries
heading to the Sunshine
Coast, points of interest in
North Vancouver such as
Capilano Suspension Bridge
and the Capilano Fish
Hatchery as well as roads
leading to Lynn Valley,
Mount Seymour and the
lovely little bay of Deep
Cove.

Tour G: False Creek

Pillow Porridge Guest House
$85-$135 bkfst incl.
tv, ℝ, K,
2859 Manitoba St.
☎879-8977
≈897-8966
www.pillow.net
The Pillow Porridge Guest
House is a residence dating
back to 1910, and the decor
and ambience attest to it.
These complete apartments
with kitchens are pleasant

and comfortable. Close to a number of ethnically diverse restaurants.

 **Chez Phillipe**
$175-$225 bkfst incl.
pb, tv, ℝ, K, P
by appointment only
☎*649-2817*

Chez Phillipe is located in the heart of Vancouver in the West End neighbourhood, two steps away from False Creek in a very holiday-like setting. It's a luxurious apartment on the 17th floor of a modern highrise built at the entrance to the Seawall. To cross False Creek to get to Granville Island Market, you can take a charming little ferry that leaves from the foot of the building. A generous breakfast is included in the price and you can even cook for yourself if you like. Guests also have access to a dishwasher, a washing machine and a dryer as well as a full bathroom with a separate shower and a terrace. By reservation only.

Tour H: Shaughnessy and South Vancouver

Stay'n Save Inn
$79
tv, K, ℝ
10551 St. Edwards Dr.
near the airport
☎*273-3311*
⇄*273-9522*

This decent facility has comfortable rooms (some of which have kitchenettes), and a family-style restaurant.

 William House
$95-$190 bkfst incl.
tv
2050 West 18th Ave.
☎/⇄*731-2760*
whouse@direct.ca

William House is a beautiful, completely restored country house in the old area of Shaughnessy, a few minutes from downtown. Luxury suites and rooms offer a pleasantly calm, comfortable environment. The large garden and yard provide havens from all the noise of the city. Well suited to business people. Prices are negotiable depending on the season and the length of your stay.

Best Western Abercorn Inn

$140

tv

9260 Bridgeport Rd., Richmond

☎*270-7576 or 800-663-0085*

⇄*270-0001*

The Best Western Abercorn Inn is relatively affordable for its category. It is located close to the airport and many shopping malls. A good choice for travellers looking for something halfway between the airport and downtown.

Radisson Hotel

150 $

≈, ℝ, ℜ, ◉, ☺, ♿, ✗

8181 Cambie Rd, Richmond

☎*276-8181 or 800-333-3333*

⇄*279-8381*

Located near the airport, the Radisson Hotel offers a high level of comfort. Rooms have coffee-makers and refrigerators, as well as work desks. Decor in the guest rooms, meeting rooms and restaurants is modern and classic, providing a relaxing atmosphere. A physical fitness centre and pool are well appreciated by some, especially during the rainy season. Next to the hotel is a very impressive Chinese supermarket; the hotel is located in Richmond, a suburb with a high percentage of Chinese residents. Upstairs from the supermarket is a Buddhist temple where visitors are received gracefully and can have the various aspects of Buddhism explained to them (see "Exploring," p. 105)

Delta Vancouver Airport Hotel and Marina

$150-$300

tv, ≈, ℜ

3500 Cessna Dr., Richmond

☎*278-1241*

☎*800-268-1133*

⇄*276-1975*

The exciting spectacle of planes and seaplanes landing is part of staying at the Delta Vancouver Airport Hotel and Marina. This hotel offers all the amenities you would expect in a hotel of the Delta chain. It is located on the edge of the airport, close to the Fraser River.

Tour I: The West Side

Vancouver International Hostel Jericho Beach

$16-$20

men's and women's dormitories

some private rooms

sb, tv, cafeteria from Apr to Oct

1515 Discovery St.

☎*224-3208*

⇄*224-4852*

Located in Jericho Park, this youth hostel is open day and night; take UBC bus #4 from downtown to reach it. With Locarno and Jericho beaches nearby, this is a great spot for budget travellers.

UBC Housing and Conference Centre
$22-$105
sb/pb, K, ℝ, P, ♿
5961 Student Union Blvd.
reservation
@brock.housing.ubc.ca
☎*822-1010*
⇋*822-1001*
In addition to a year-round 48-suite hotel, campus apartments are available from May to August. Inexpensive and well located near museums, beaches and hiking trails, this spot also provides tranquillity.

Johnson House Bed & Breakfast
$80-$155 bkfst incl.
sb/pb
Nov to Feb by request only
2278 West 34th Ave. Kerrisdale district
☎/ ⇋*266-4175*
www.johnsons-inn-vancouver.com
The Johnson House Bed & Breakfast occupies a magnificent, fully renovated house from the 1920s with an extra floor added. The owners, Sandy and Ron Johnson, carried out the work and also acquired several antiques that form part of the decor.

Plaza 500 Hotel
$109
tv, ☉, ℜ
500 West 12th Ave., corner of Cambie St.
☎*873-1811*
⇋*873-1980*
Located 15min by car from downtown just after the Cambie bridge, this beautiful hotel has sumptuous rooms and view of the city. Broadway Street, only 2min away, has a variety of shops, restaurants and bars. The perfect place for large groups or conferences -- why here as well as earlier? In right place???.

Penny Farthing Inn Bed & Breakfast
$115-170 bkfst incl.
sb or pb
2855 West Sixth Avenue, Kitsilano
☎*739-9002*
⇋*739-9004*
farthing@uniserve.com
Lyn Hairstock receives you warmly in her home built in 1912. Wood and stained glass give the four rooms plenty of charm. Smoking not allowed.

Restaurants

I n this chapter
you will find a multitude of great restaurants where you can satisfy your hunger, enjoy a great meal or simply sample the region's specialties.

Restaurants by Type of Cuisine

Cafes and Tea Rooms

Canadian

Chinese

West Coast

Steamworks Brewing
    Co., p 153
The Raintree, p 153
A Kettle of Fish, p 166
Chartwell, p 162
Byron's Grill, p 161

Spanish and Mexican

Sienna Tapas Bar
    & Grill, p 169
Bin 941, p 164
Tapastree, p 161
Primo's Mexican
    Grill, p 169

French

L'Etoile, p 166
Le Café de Paris, p 161
The Smoking Dog, p 169

Seafood
Amorous Oyster, p 167

Greek

Maria's Taverna, p 169

Indian
India Village, p 152
Jewel of India, p 152

Italian

The Old Spaghetti
    Factory, p 152
Capone's, p 156
Il Giardino, p 165
Goodfellas, p 160

Japanese

Kitto, p 155
Furosato, p 155

Breakfast

Epicurean Caffe, p 168
Gypsy Rose, p 167

Tour A: Gastown

The Old Spaghetti Factory
$
53 Water St.
☎*684-1288*
With posters and photogra-
phy on the walls and a cozy
atmosphere, this restaurant
serves up all kinds of Italian
pasta at reasonable prices.
The menu includes hot
bread, salad and ice cream.

India Village
$$
308 Water St.
☎*681-0678*
As you enjoy carefully pre-
pared, authentic Indian
cuisine from your table, you
can admire the 19th-century
steam-powered clock, as
well as the hectic pace of
the centre of Gastown, an
area typical of the period.

Jewel of India
$$
52 Alexander St.
☎*687-5665*
This restaurant excels at
making nan bread in its
clay ovens, which perfectly
accompany the popular,
traditional Tandoori dishes.

Steamworks Brewing Co
$$$
375 Water St.
☎*689-2739*
Enjoy some regional West Coast cuisine with your favourite beer, which is brewed on the premises.

The Raintree
$$$
375 Water St.
☎*689-2739*
With its beautiful, friendly dining room, this restaurant offers West Coast cuisine. Some interesting specialities are made with regional products, such as its famous leg of lamb. Impressive wine list. This restaurant was honoured by a visit from President Clinton during his last visit to Vancouver.

Top of Vancouver
$$$
*Sunday brunch buffet for $26.95
every day 11:30am to 2:30pm and 5pm to 10pm
except Sun brunch at 11am*
555 West Hastings St.
☎*669-2220*
This restaurant, located atop Harbour Centre (the elevator is free for restaurant patrons), revolves once an hour, giving diners a city tour from high in the air while they eat. Classic West Coast cuisine is served here.

Water Street Cafe
$$$
300 Water St.
☎*689-2832*
The freshly baked bread that comes from the ovens of the Water Street Cafe accompanies the pasta and fish dishes. This contemporary-style restaurant has a laid-back, friendly ambience.

Tour B: Chinatown and East Vancouver

Restaurants

Gain Wah Down
$
218 Keefer St.
☎*684-1740*
Treat yourself to crab, roasted chicken with tofu or the unique flavour of andouillette (a small sausage). Family-style quality cuisine.

Hon's Wun-Tun House
$
268 Keefer St.
☎*688-8303*
This restaurant has been a Vancouver institution for more than 20 years. Its reasonably priced dishes, including traditional Chinese specialities, are all excellent. Sample some of the dishes in the noisy, jam-packed, canteen-style atmosphere. Efficient service.

Joe's Café
$
1150 Commercial Dr.
This spot is frequented by a regular clientele of intellectuals, Sunday philosophers and feminists, among others. What brings them together, most of all, is Joe's coffee.

Kam Gok Yuen
$
142 East Pender St.
☎*683-3822*
This restaurant has a vast selection of mouth-watering dishes, such as Peking duck, which are often advertised in Chinese on the walls.

Waa Zuu Bee Café
$
every day 11:30am to 1am
1622 Commercial Dr.
☎*253-5299*
The Waa Zuu Bee Café is great and inexpensive. The innovative cuisine combined with the "natural-techno-italo-bizarre" decor are full of surprises. The pasta dishes are always interesting.

Nick's Spaghetti House
$-$$
631 Commercial Dr.
☎*254-5633*
Copious meals are served on red-and-white-checked tablecloths amidst landscape paintings of Capri and Sorrento. People are friendly here and patrons enter the restaurant through

the kitchen, a reassuring element.

Park Lock
$$
544 Main St.
☎*688-1581*
The Park Lock, which features traditional Cantonese cuisine, is a Vancouver institution. Shrimp, steak and pork chops are its specialities.

Santos Tapas Restaurant
$$
1191 Commercial Dr.
☎*253-0444*
Latinos seem to have a gift for calming the atmosphere with the aromas of their spices and with their music. This is certainly the case here where groups of musicians perform at your table. This restaurant is frequented mostly by Vancouverites.

Sun Sui Wah Seafood Restaurant
$$
every day
3888 Main St., at Third Ave.
☎*872-8822*
Authentic Chinese food, lobster, crayfish, crab, oysters and, of course, Peking duck.

Cannery Seafood Restaurant
$$$
until 10pm
2205 Commissioner St.
☎*254-9606*
The Cannery Seafood Restaurant is one of the best

places in town for seafood. It is located in the East End in a renovated, century-old warehouse. The view of the sea is fantastic.

Tour C: Downtown

DV8
$
515 Davie St.
☎*682-4388*
The DV8 is a café.

Dining Car
$
Mon to Fri noon to 2:30pm, Fri and Sat 5pm to 2am
at the Railway Club
579 Dunsmuir St.
☎*681-1625*
A relaxing ambience and family-style fare are served up at the Dining Car, where the clientele runs the gamut from suits to artists.

Furosato
$
616 Davie St.
corner Seymore St.
☎*682-5494*
Located on the outskirts of downtown and in the new, hip Yaletown area, sushi, robata and other Japanese specialities are served up in this small restaurant that also delivers.

India Gate
$
616 Robson St.
☎*684-4617*
You can get a curry dish for as little as $5.95 at lunch-time. In the evening, this restaurant is rather deserted. The decor is not at all exotic.

Kitto
$
833 Granville St.
☎*687-6622*
All kinds of Japanese delicacies such as *sushi, robata* and *yakisoba*. Reasonable prices and fast service.

Malone's Bar & Grill
$
every day
608 West Pender St.
☎*684-9977*
You can enjoy steak, salmon, chicken, pizza or beer, all reasonably priced, while watching a hockey game on their giant screen. Music and Cuban cigars.

Maverick's
$
770 Pacific Blvd, Plaza of Nations
☎*683-4436*
This grill, which has dances on the weekends, serves up steak and beer while you watch your favourite game on the big screen.

White Spot
$
580 West Georgia St.
☎*662-3066*
This restaurant belongs to the White Spot chain of restaurants established in the 1920s. A Vancouver institution, this family-style restaurant still has a great reputation and comfortable

Restaurants

atmosphere. Its Triple O Hamburger has been and remains the all-time favourite of several generations.

Arena Ristorante
$$
11:30am to 2:30pm and 5pm to 10pm
300 West Georgia St.
☎*687-5434*
The Arena Ristorante serves Italian specialties. The atmosphere is livelier on Friday and Saturday nights when live jazz performances are put on.

Bacchus Restaurant
$$
Wedgewood Hotel
845 Hornby St.
☎*689-7777*
A lovely, intimate decor, an ambience enhanced by piano music and a cuisine cooked up by an award-winning chef make this restaurant popular with its downtown clientele.

Capone's
$$
1141 Hamilton St.
☎*682-7900*
This romantic restaurant has a New Orleans-style atmosphere with a jazz orchestra. It serves intimate candlelight diners including pizza, pasta or salads, accompanied with a selection of original martinis. Located in the trendy new area of Yaletown.

Dix Barbecue and Brewery
$$
871 Beatty St.
☎*682-2739*
Reasonably priced grills and beer are served up in a youthful, laid-back atmosphere.

Hard Rock Café
$$
until 1am
686 West Hastings St.
☎*687-ROCK*
The Hard Rock Café is part of the famous worldwide chain of restaurants where paraphernalia from famous rock stars and Harley Davidson gadgets decorate the walls, and delicious burgers and nachos are served.

Planet Hollywood
$$
every day
969 Robson St.
☎*688-7827*
The theme of the decor is television and film. They show movies and a lot of advertising on giant screens and offer a simple menu: burgers, fries and drinks. T-shirts and gadgets are for sale in the boutique. Worth investigating only if you've never been to a Planet Hollywood.

Rodney's Oyster House
$$
1228 Hamilton St.
☎*609-0080*
This restaurant's boat-style decor gives it a maritime

feeling. Its fish and fresh seafood soups are presented in large bowls and served up with a smile.

Settebello
$$

1133 Robson St.
☎*681-7377*

Stettebello serves pizzas and salads with olive oil and Italian bread, a warm ambiance as well as a lovely dining room and a terrace decorated with flowers.

Tsunami Sushi
$$

238-1025 Robson St.
☎*687-8744, unit 238*

Tsunami Sushi has a revolving sushi bar, much like those in Japan, from which patrons can choose specialties at will. Excellent quality for the price. Huge, sunny terrace overlooking Robson Street.

Yaletown Brewing Co.
$$

closed midnight
1111 Mainland St.
☎*681-2739*

The Yaletown Brewing Co. is a veritable yuppie temple in the post-industrial neighbourhood of Yaletown and a fun place to spend an evening. Try the pizza from the wood-burning oven.

Aqua Riva
$$$

200 Granville St.
in front of the Waterfront Hotel
☎*683-5599*

Enjoy roasts and grills cooked on a wood fire in a colourful ambience with a magnificent view of the ocean.

Diva at the Met
$$$

645 Howe St.
☎*602-7788*

Decent continental cuisine and fine wine served up in a pleasant ambience with elegant decor. A popular restaurant with Vancouver's jet set.

Joe Fortes
$$$

777 Thurlow St., at Robson
☎*669-1940*

Joe Fortes is renowned in the West End for its oysters and other seafood. With its turn-of-the-century decor and heated upstairs terrace, this bistro has an appetizing menu. This is a popular meeting place for successful young professionals.

Imperial
$$$-$$$$

Mon to Fri 11am to 2:30pm and 5pm to 10pm
Sat and Sun and holidays 10:30am to 2:30pm and 5pm to 10pm
355 Burrard St.
☎*688-8191*

Located in the Marine Building, an Art Deco archi-

Restaurants

tectural masterpiece (see p 74), this Chinese restaurant also has several Art Deco elements. It is the big windows looking over Burrard Inlet, however, that are especially fascinating. In this very elegant spot, boys in livery and discreet young ladies perform the *dim sum* ritual. Unlike elsewhere, there are no carts here: the various steamed dishes are brought on trays. You can also ask for a list, allowing you to choose your favourites among the 30 or so offered. The quality of the food matches the excellent reputation this restaurant has acquired.

Le Crocodile
$$$-$$$$
909 Burrard St.
entry by Smithe St.
☎669-4298

This establishment is the beacon of French cuisine in Vancouver as much for the quality of its food as for its service, its decor and its wine list. Lovers of great French cuisine will be spoiled by the choice of red meats and the delicacies from the sea. The salmon tartare is a must – you *are* on the Pacific coast after all!

Tour D: The West End

Bino's
$
885 West Broadway
☎874-7415
2126 West Broadway
☎733-6316
2001 Lonsdale Ave., North Vancouver
☎985-4516
Bino's restaurants serve crepes and Canadian cuisine.

Bread Garden
$
24hrs/day
1040 Denman St.
☎685-2996
812 Bute St.
☎688-3213
2996 Granville St.
☎736-6465
These cafés sell bread, pastries and tasty prepared dishes to go, such as quiches, lasagnas, sandwiches, and fruit plates. Good vegetarian selections. You can also enjoy all of these in-house. Good service and low prices. Also located at:
1880 West First Ave., Kitsilano
☎738-6684
550 Park Royal N., West Vancouver
☎925-0181
4575 Central Blvd., Burnaby
☎435-5177

Ciao Espresso Bar
$
1074 Denman St.
☎682-0112
Folks come to this little West End establishment for the strong, dark brew and the neighbourhood atmosphere.

Da Pasta Bar
$
1232 Robson St.
☎688-1288
This Italian restaurant, located in the most refined part of Robson Street, offers original items such as pasta with curry. Full lunches for $7.50. Pleasant decor.

Flying Wedge Pizza Co.
$
Royal Centre
1055 W. Georgia St.
☎681-1233
3499 Cambie St.
☎874-8284
1937 Cornwall, Kitsilano
☎732-8840
Vancouver Airport
☎303-3370
Library Square
☎689-7078
For pizza lovers, these are addresses to jot down if you're looking for pizza that doesn't remind you of something you ate last week. You'll get a discount if you bring your own plate, showing that you're ecologically minded.

Fresgo Inn Restaurant & Bakery
$
1138 Davie St.
☎689-1332
The Fresgo Inn Restaurant & Bakery is fairly renowned for its portions and prices.

La Crêpe Bretonne
$
795 Jervis St.
☎608-1266
At La Crêpe Bretonne, you can enjoy a large variety of crepes – with sugar, eggs, ham or chicken – all to the sound of French songs hummed by the owner. Worth a visit.

Starbucks
$
1099 Robson St.
☎685-1099
A green logo marks the spot. Capuccino, espresso, big, small, medium, strong, weak, decaf, with milk, cold with chocolate or nutmeg: the choice is yours. Charming terrace. Several other branches of this Seattle-based chain are scattered around Vancouver and surrounding areas

True Confections
$
until 1am
866 Denman St.
☎682-1292
True Confections is a dessert place par excellence that serves huge slices of cake. Be sure to try the divine Belgian dark chocolate torte.

Restaurants

Ohana Sushi
$-$$
1414 West Broadway
☎ *732-0112*
This chain of Japanese restaurants offers excellent dishes at reasonable prices. Service is efficient and pleasant. A fine Asian experience.

Sakae Japanese Restaurant
$-$$ for lunch
745 Thurlow St.
☎ *669-0067*
It is easy to walk right past this restaurant, situated in the basement of a commercial building. But the welcoming smiles and the quality of the food compensate for its location. The sushi and sashimi will literally melt in your mouth.

Goodfellas
$$
1166 Alberni St.
☎ *689-3370*
Pasta, pizza, veal, smoked breast of duck and other Italian specialities are served up in a beautiful dining room furnished with varnished wood panelling. Elegant setting and pleasant atmosphere. Live jazz every evening.

 Gyoza King
$$
1508 Robson St.
☎ *669-8278*
The items served here range from teriyaki dishes to sashimi and include the chef's specialties such as

marinated anchovies. Warm atmosphere.

Liliget
$$
every day
1724 Davie St.
☎ *681-7044*
Liliget is a First Nations restaurant that offers authentic Aboriginal-style food: salmon grilled on a wood fire, smoked oysters, grilled seaweed and roasted wild duck. Worth exploring.

Marbella
$$
1368 Robson St.
☎ *681-1175*
Marbella is a Spanish restaurant largely frequented by tourists. They serve excellent garlic shrimp with *margaritas*, various salads, tapas and, notably, real paella. Spanish guitarists and dancers on Thursdays and Fridays.

Mescallero
$$
until midnight weekdays
1am weekends
1215 Bidwell St.
☎ *669-2399*
The Latin-American and Mexican cuisine of Mescallero is served in a pretty setting with a friendly ambience. Things get really busy on Saturday evenings.

...nley Park is filled with flowering gardens, adding a splash of colour to this much-cherished green space. - *Tibor Bognàr*

Scores of yachts and sailboats flock to Coal Harbour Bay,
augmenting the West End's seaside charm. - *Troy & Mary Parlee*

🚢 Miko Sushi
$$
Mon to Sat
1335 Robson St.
☎*681-0339*
Meticulously prepared Japanese food; extremely fresh sushi and sashimi; impeccable service in this small restaurant. Reservations recommended.

Milestone's
$$
1210 Denman St.
☎*662-3431*
The hamburger plates, steaks and salads come in generous portions. Freshly-squeezed fruit juices. Lovely terrace facing English Bay.

Moose's
$$
630 W. Pender St.
☎*683-3300*
This Canadian-style pub-restaurant serves up generous portions of steak, spaghetti, fries and much more. Convivial atmosphere.

🚢 Raku
$$
838 Thurlow St., north of Robson
☎*685-8817*
A wealthy young Japanese clientele meets here and fits right in. It has the atmosphere of a noisy bar, but it is an ideal spot to begin a promising evening. The sushi and grilled meats are recommended.

Tapastree
$$
1829 Robson St.
☎*606-4280*
A selection of tapas and grilled lamb.

TGI Friday's
$$
803 Thurlow St., corner Robson St.
☎*682-6422*
More than a hundred tasty dishes and a great selection of drinks in this fast-food-style North American family restaurant. Terrace with a view of Robson Street

Ballantine's Restaurant
$$$
432 Richards St.
☎*689-2700*
Ballantine's serves up great continental cuisine in a stunning decor. Efficient service.

Byron's Grill
$$$
1160 Davie St., Parkhill Hotel
☎*685-1311, extension 2573*
The buffet at Byron's Grill has an excellent selection of quality food. Crab, shrimp, sushi, salmon and other dishes will satiate your appetite. On weekends, a hip DJ will get you dancing.

🚢 Le Café de Paris
$$$
751 Denman St.
☎*687-1418*
The speciality of Le Café de Paris is its *cassoulet* (a stew originating from southwestern France). Many other

Restaurants

dishes are inspired from different regions of France. The fries that accompany every dish are excellent. Good wine and prompt service.

Raincity Grill
$$$
until 10:30pm
1139 Denman St.
☎685-7337
The Raincity Grill specializes in grilled fish and meats in true West Coast tradition. A bit pricey.

Rex Rotisserie & Grill
$$$
1055 Dunsmuir St., Bentall Centre
☎683-7390
American-style grill with a patio and a pleasant ambience.

The Old Bailiff
$$$
800 Robson, Robson Square
☎684-7448
An English-style pub atmosphere with a patio and traditional Canadian fare.

L'Hermitage
$$$-$$$$
every day
1025 Robson St., Suite 115
☎689-3237
The chef-owner Hervé Martin is an artist when it comes to French cuisine. He will tell you stories from his days as the chef of the Belgian Royal Court. Wines from his native region of Burgundy accompany the finest of dishes, each prepared carefully and with panache. The decor is chic and the service exemplary. The terrace, set back from Robson, is lovely in the summertime.

Chartwell
$$$$
791 West Georgia St.
☎844-6715
Chartwell has won several awards. The service is impeccable and the cuisine has West Coast influences.

Cloud 9 Revolving Restaurant
$$$$
until 11pm
1400 Robson St.
☎687-0511
The Cloud 9 Revolving Restaurant is an experience. This resto-bar at the top of the 40-storey Landmark Hotel (see p 144) offers an exceptional view. It takes 80min for the restaurant to rotate 360°. Sunset is particularly picturesque as the sky darkens and the city begins to glow. Try the lamb chops or the salmon.

Le Gavroche
$$$$
evenings every day and mornings Mon to Fri
1616 Alberni St.
☎685-3924
Fine French cuisine in a Victorian house. Reservations required.

Tour E: Stanley Park

Prospect Point Café
$
Stanley Park
☎669-2737
The Prospect Point Café is located at the historical observation site on the tip of Stanley Park. You can contemplate Lions Gate Bridge at sunset and sample steaks, pasta and chicken burgers.

The Fish House in Stanley Park
$$$
until 10:30pm
8901 Stanley Park Dr.
☎681-7275
The Fish House in Stanley Park is located in a Victorian house right in the heart of the park and just a few steps from the Seawall. Fine seafood and fish dishes are served in a lovely, opulent decor.

Teahouse Restaurant
$$$
until 10pm
along the Seawall
7501 Stanley Park Dr.
☎669-3281
The Teahouse Restaurant serves delicious food and offers stunning views of English Bay from Stanley Park. Call ahead for reservations and for precise directions as it can be tricky to find.

Tour F: Burrard Inlet

Bean Around the World
$
1522 Marine Dr., West Vancouver
☎925-9600
A crowd of rather laid-back people squeezes into this warm spot. Excellent coffees and sweets are served at reasonable prices.

Beach Side Café
$$
11am to 3:30pm and 5:30pm to 11:30pm
1362 Marine Dr.
☎925-1945
The Beach Side Café in West Vancouver is a lovely restaurant with original recipes prepared from local produce, as well as meat and fish dishes.

Boathouse
$$
until 9:30pm, 10pm weekends
6695 Nelson Ave., Horseshoe Bay
☎921-8188
The Boathouse is a large glassed-in restaurant at the heart of the quaint community of Horseshoe Bay. Seafood is its specialty: oysters, halibut, salmon...

Bridge House Restaurant
$$
brunch 11am to 2pm
3735 Capilano Rd.
North Vancouver
☎987-3388
In a warm and intimate English-style setting, this

Restaurants

restaurant serves traditional Canadian dishes, home-made pies and warm bread. Reservations recommended.

The Salmon House on the Hill
$$$
every day
2229 Folkestone Way
West Vancouver
☎926-8539
www.salmonhouse.com
The Salmon House offers unique, creative cuisine that focuses on salmon in a superb, Canadian-cedar decor. A view of the ocean, the city and Stanley Park adds to the pleasure of the palate.

Tour G: False Creek

Bin 941
$
941 Davie St.
☎683-1246
Tapas and tasty West Coast dishes.

La Baguette et L'Échalotte
$
8am to 6pm
1680 Johnston St.
☎684-1351
If you expect to be picnicking during your visit to Granville Island, here is where you will find French bread, pastries, croissants and take-out dishes. Louise and Mario take good care of this little shop, located in the heart of busy Granville Island.

Bridges Bistro
$
until 11:30pm
1696 Duranleau St.
Granville Island
☎687-4400
≈687-0352
The Bridges Bistro boasts one of the prettiest terraces in Vancouver, right by the water in the middle of Granville Island's pleasure-boat harbour. The food and setting are decidedly West Coast.

Chateau Madrid - La Bodega
$$
closed Sun and holidays
1277 Howe St.
☎684-8814
Restaurant and tapas bar; traditional paella and sangria.

The Creek Restaurant & Brewery
$$
Granville Island
1253 Johnston St.
☎685-7070
This enormous elegant restaurant has a patio as well as a great view of the False Creek sailing harbour. It offers both simple and more elaborate dishes, all meticulously presented. Open late. Two adjoining bars serve several different kinds of beer, such as the famous Granville Island Pale Ale. All are brewed on the premises. Connected to a nightclub (open on weekends).

Kamei Royale Ocean
$$
1333 Johnston St., Granville Island
☎*602-0005*
Kamei Royale Ocean is a conveniently located and lovely restaurant. Sushi, sashimi, *miso* and teriyaki are the house specialties. It offers a wonderful view overlooking the cove. Fast service.

The Keg
$$
until 10pm,
midnight weekends
1499 Anderson St., Granville Island
☎*685-4735*
Meat-eaters converge on The Keg. There are lots of steaks to choose from and prices are reasonable. The atmosphere is relaxed and the staff particularly friendly.

Monk McQueens
$$
every day
601 Stamps Landing
☎*877-1351*
Specialties are fish and an oyster buffet. This restaurant overlooks the inlet and has the decor of a small sailing club. Very pleasant inside and on the terrace. Impeccable service and delicious food. A pianist accompanies your meal.

Panama Jacks Bar and Grill
$$
1080 Howe St.
☎*682-5225*
This restaurant has a ter-race, colourful decor and friendly ambience. Standard fare and pizza. Open late.

C
$$$
1600 Howe St.
☎*605-8263*
This Chinese restaurant, whose name evokes the sea, is the talk of the town, and for good reason. The chef has returned from Southeast Asia with innova-tive and unique recipes. Served on the stroke of 12, the C-style Dim Sum is a real delight. Titbits of fish marinated in tea and a touch of caviar, vol-au-vents with chanterelles, curry shrimp with coconut milk, and the list goes on... All quite simply exquisite. Des-serts are equally extraordi-nary. For those who dare, the crème brûlée with blue cheese is an unforgettable experience. This restaurant is an absolute must.

Il Giardino
$$$
1382 Hornby St.
☎*669-2422*
This popular restaurant has a renowned reputation for its attractive Italian-style decor, charming patio, in-spired dishes with local and European accents and its vast selection of Italian pasta. Always crowded. Warm, friendly ambience.

Kettle of Fish
$$$
900 Pacific St.
☎682-6661
Kettle of fish has a cosy winter garden-style ambience with flowers. The menu includes tasty fish and fresh seafood as well as an excellent wine list. Good service.

Pacific Institute of Culinary Arts
$$$
1505 West Second Ave.
☎734-4488
The Pacific Institute of Culinary Arts has a patio and offers a different gourmet menu every day prepared by its students. The dishes are exquisite and the service is excellent.

L'Etoile
$$$$
1355 Hornby Street
☎661-4444
With a classic, elegant decor, this restaurant offers meticulously prepared contemporary French cuisine, accompanied by an excellent choice of wines. Impeccable service.

Tour H: Shaughnessy and South Vancouver

Big News Coffee Bar
$
2447 Granville St., at Broadway
☎739-7320
The Big News Coffee Bar, an alternative to Starbucks, is a pleasant neighbourhood café. The decor is modern and sober and they offer fast service, good coffee and a number of magazines and newspapers to leaf through while you eat.

Ohana Sushi
$-$$
1414 West Broadway
☎732-0112
This chain of Japanese restaurants offers excellent dishes at reasonable prices. Service is efficient and pleasant. A fine Asian experience.

Landmark Hotpot House
$$
4023 Cambie St.
☎872-2868
The Landmark Hotpot House is one of the best hotpot restaurants in Vancouver. (Hotpots are meat or fish dishes sautéed in hot casseroles.) This popular restaurant is always packed. It cooks up a variety of soups, such as chicken or meat, accompanied with vegetables and original

sauces such as *satay*, the house special.

Royal Seoul House Korean Restaurant
$$
1215 West Broadway
☎*738-8285* or *739-9001*
The Royal Seoul House Korean Restaurant has a large dining room divided into compartments. Each has a table with a grill for preparing food that can accommodate four or more people. Order your all-you-can-eat meat, fish and seafood buffet, and have fun. Everything here is good, including the service.

Amorous Oyster
$$$
3236 Oak St.
☎*732-5916*
This restaurant offers a great selection of West Coast-style dishes for fish and seafood lovers.

Seasons in the Park
$$$-$$$$
right in Queen Elizabeth Park
33 Cambie St.
☎*874-8008*
Seasons in the Park is a pleasant restaurant with classic, elegant decor and an unhindered view of the city. Succulent cuisine. Reservations required.

Tour I: The West Side

De Dutch Pannekoek House
$
2622 Granville St.
☎*731-0775*
De Dutch Pannekoek House is a specialist in pancake breakfasts. Big beautiful pancakes are made to order, plain or with your favourite fillings. There are about ten of these restaurants, including one at 1725 Robson Street and another at 1260 Davie. The one on Granville is calm and pleasant, and the service is perfect.

Gypsy Rose
$
1660 Cypress St.
☎*731-3528*
A little cafe situated on a street with many shops, Gypsy Rose offers pastries, light fare and specialities from southern France. Bernard, the friendly manager, is from Marseille.

Naam
$
24hrs/day
2724 West Fourth Ave.
☎*738-7151*
The Naam blends live music with vegetarian meals. This little restaurant has a warm atmosphere, friendly service, and is frequented by a young clientele.

Restaurants

🦑 Pâtisserie Lebeau
$
1660 Cypress St.
☎ *731-3528*
This quaint little place, which has a few chairs outside, bakes delicious cakes. It serves up hot waffles for breakfast and scrumptious sandwiches for lunch (such as ham and cheese on a French baguette) accompanied by coffee and a lively atmosphere. Try the Liège waffles. Practice your French with Olivier, the Belgian owner, who makes all the delectable pastry.

Sophie's Cosmic Café
$
2095 West Fourth Ave.
☎ *732-6810*
This is a weekend meeting-spot for the Kitsilano crowd, who come to stuff themselves with bacon and eggs. 1950s decor, relaxed atmosphere.

The Vineyard
$
2296 West Fourth Ave.
☎ *733-2420*
The Vineyard serves Greek specialties.

🦑 Epicurean Caffe
$$
1898 West First Ave.
corner Cypress St.
☎ *731-5370*
Owners Dario and his son Christian serve Italian-style cuisine. Chose the dish and the portion you desire on the home-made menu. With a friendly warm atmosphere, this quaint little place whips up one of the best expressos in Vancouver. Bask in the winter or summer sun at one of the outdoor tables. The motorcycles and bikes parked along the sidewalk are a hot topic of conversation amongst the regulars.

Fiction
$$
3162 West Broadway
☎ *736-7576*
Fiction is a long, New York-style bar with a convivial atmosphere that specializes in tapas.

Japanese Bistro Kitsilano
$$
1815 West First Ave.
☎ *734-5858*
Japanese Bistro Kitsilano features an all-you-can-eat sushi and tempura buffet. Large terrace and excellent service.

Las Margaritas
$$
until 10pm, 11pm weekends
1999 West Fourth Ave.
☎ *734-7117*
Las Margaritas serves healthy Mexican fare in a lively setting with lots of ambience. A great place to go with a group of friends.

Maria's Taverna
$$
2324 West Fourth Ave.
☎*731-4722*
This pretty little restaurant serves up generous portions of authentic Greek cuisine in a blue-checked decor. The roast lamb is highly recommended.

Mark's Steak and Tap House
$$
until 1am
2486 Bayswater St.
☎*734-1325*
Mark's Steak and Tap House is a yuppie hangout on the West Side whose parking lot is filled with Harleys on a regular basis. The food is Italian with pastas, pizzas, and the mood is relaxed with jazz in the evenings.

Ouisi Bistro
$$
3014 Granville St.
☎*732-7550*
This quaint little New Orleans-style restaurant has a charming atmosphere with live jazz. Original and creative menu.

Primo's Mexican Grill
$$
1509 West 12th Ave.
☎*736-9322*
Primo's Mexican Grill serves up all kinds of tasty Mexican dishes in a laid-back, friendly atmosphere. A good selection of tasty margaritas.

Sienna Tapas Bar & Grill
$$
1809 West First Ave.
☎*738-2727*
In its large, contemporary dining room, Sienna Tapas Bar & Grill prepares all kinds of tapas, pasta and many other tasty little dishes.

The Smoking Dog
$$
1889 West First Ave.
☎*736-8811*
The Smoking Dog has a warm, lively atmosphere, lovely decor and reasonable prices for its carefully prepared *table d'hôte*. Exquisite steak, copious salads and creative daily specials. The fries that accompany every dish are golden brown on the outside and tender on the inside. Jean-Claude, the owner, is a friendly *Marseillais*.

Raku Kushiyaki Restaurant
$$-$$$
closed Mon
4422 West 10th Ave.
☎*222-8188*
The young chefs of this little restaurant prepare local cuisine served with oriental aesthetic rules in mind; they will help you discover their art. Take a meal for two to appreciate the spirit of this *nouvelle cuisine* which encourages the sharing of meals among guests. The portions may seem small, but you still come away satiated. Ingre-

Restaurants

dients are chosen according to the seasons. For example wild mushrooms are served accented with garlic, green bell peppers, butter, soya sauce and lime juice. This dish may seem simple, and it is, but the taste of the food is not masked by mediocre sauces. The meat and fish are also treated with subtlety.

Wild Garlic
$$$
2120 West Broadway
☎ *730-0880*
Wild Garlic serves up this herb every way imaginable, and also offers traditional Canadian cuisine. Meticulous, stylish setting and friendly, attentive service.

Lumière
$$$$
closed Mon
2551 West Broadway
☎ *739-8185*
Lumière is a favourite with Vancouver residents, especially chefs. The simple, white interior allows the food to shine, and shine it does! The fresh, local ingredients used in each dish make for creative and honest, yet very refined cuisine. One winning choice is veal tenderloin with braised turnip lasagna topped off by lemon tarts or chocolate truffles.

Star Anise
$$$$
every day 5:30pm to 11pm, and Tue to Fri 11:30am to 2pm
1485 West 12th Ave.
☎ *737-1485*
Star Anise is a very pretty and stylish restaurant frequented by the beautiful people. Big paintings adorn the yellow walls, and lanterns illuminate the tables.

Entertainment

ARTS Hotline
(☎684-ARTS) will inform you about all
the shows (dance, theatre, music, cinema
and literature) in the
city.

The Georgia Straight
(☎730-7000). This
weekly paper is published
every Thursday and distrib-
uted free at many spots in
Vancouver. You will find
all the necessary information on coming shows and
cultural events. This paper
is read religiously each
week by many
Vancouverites and has ac-
quired a good reputation.

For information on jazz
shows in Vancouver,
call the **Jazz Hotline**
(☎682-0706).

To book tickets for cultural or sporting events,
try the following:

Ticketmaster
☎280-4444

Arts Line
☎280-3311 *(for tickets only)*

Sports Line
☎280-4400

Bars and Nightclubs by Type

Comedy Clubs

Rhythm and Blues Bars

Jazz Clubs

Nightclubs

Nightclubs (continued)

Gay and Lesbian Bars

Pool Halls

Pubs

Bars and Nightclubs

Tour A: Gastown

Blarney Stone
216 Carrall St.
☎ **687-4322**
The Blarney Stone is the spot for authentic Irish jigs and reels. The ambience is frenetic, with people dancing everywhere – on the tables, on the chairs... A must-see!

Lamplighter's Bar
210 Abbott St.
☎ **681-6666**
A diverse assortment of people frequent this unpretentious bar. Local blues bands play here.

The Purple Onion Cabaret
every day
15 Water St., Third floor
☎ **602-9442**
The Purple Onion Cabaret is the mecca of upbeat jazz in Vancouver, with entertainment provided by a disc-jockey or live bands. Cover charge of $5 during the week and $7 on weekends. Wednesdays are dedicated to Latin jazz; on Fridays and Saturdays there's live jazz near the bar and "disco-funk" on the dance floor.

Rossini's Gastown
162 Water St.
☎ **408-1300**
The owner of Rossini's (see p 179) just opened a second location on the busiest street in Gastown. It serves good beer, pasta and meat, accompanied to the sounds of a live jazz singer every evening.

Sonar
66 Water St.
☎ **683-6695**
Alternative and underground DJ format with some live shows on this Gastown stage. The place is very big, and you can also play pool.

Tour B: Chinatown and East Vancouver

Hot Jazz Society
2120 Main St.
☎ **873-4131**
The Hot Jazz Society was one of the first places in Vancouver to offer good jazz. It's a veritable institution, where many of the big names in jazz perform. Call to find out who's playing.

Royal Diamond Casino
750 Pacific Blvd. S.
☎ **685-2340**
If you're feeling lucky, try your hand at the Royal Diamond Casino. Casinos in British Columbia are government owned and all the winnings are donated to charity. A good system!

Tour C: Downtown

Athletic Billiards Café
1011 Hamilton St.
☎669-3533
Located downtown at the edge of Yaletown, Athletic Billiards Café attracts a hip, young clientele. Good pool tables.

Automotive Billiards Club
1095 Homer St.
☎682-0040
Very good music, excellent pool tables and great expresso. They also serve sandwiches. There's a small divider separating the pool-table area from the bar corner. Also, it's one of the rare pool halls to serve beer. Hip, friendly atmosphere on weekends.

Babalu
654 Nelson St.
at Granville St.
☎605-4343
is a lounge-style bar. It's the ideal spot to sip a cocktail while enjoying a little Frank Sinatra and a cigar. There is also dancing to jazzy rhythms. Cover charge of $3.

Bar None
1222 Hamilton St.
☎689-7000
Bar None is the hang-out of Vancouver's trendy youth. A friendly pub atmosphere is complemented by a dance floor.

Watch out for long line-ups on Friday and Saturday evenings.

Cascades Lounge
Pan Pacific Hotel
300-999 Canada Place Way
☎662-8111
The Cascades Lounge, in the luxurious Pan Pacific Hotel, has a calm, refined ambience with sumptuous armchairs. Sip on wine or liqueurs as you listen to live guitar or piano music.

Chameleon Urban Lounge
every day
801 West Georgia St.
☎669-0806
This excellent little downtown club is often packed on weekends, but it is calm during the week. Don't miss their trip-hop nights on Wednesdays, Afro-Cuban and Latin music on Thursdays, and Acid Jazz on Saturdays. Warning: get there early to avoid lineups. The cover charge is $5 on Fridays and Saturdays.

Club Millennium
closed Sun
595 Hornby St.
☎684-2000
This Las Vegas-style nightclub has a variety of musical entertainment.

Deniro's Supper Club
1039 Mainland
☎684-2777
Deniro's Supper Club is a retro-style, modern restaurant-cabaret with a

Entertainment

charming ambience. Great pasta specials Mondays and Tuesdays.

Fred's Tavern
1006 Granville St.
☎ 605-4350
Fred's Tavern has giant screens and a warm atmosphere. The DJ plays "nostalgic" music from the '80s.

Georgia Street Bar & Grill
801 West Georgia St.
☎ 602-0994
This bar is really popular with its downtown regulars. Its well-dressed clientele flocks here in the evening to guzzle down beer, nibble on grilled dishes and listen to live jazz.

Jolly Taxpayer
828 West Hastings St.
☎ 681-3574
Located in the heart of the business district, this traditional pub is renowned for its great beer.

Lava Lounge
1176 Granville St.
☎ 605-1154
The Lava Lounge's DJ livens up the evening with swing and jazz music.

Luv-a-Fair
1275 Seymour St.
☎ 685-3288
For a heady night of techno and alternative music and dancing, check out Luv-a-Fair. Young crowd.

Madison's Nightspot
Wed to Sat
398 Richards St.
☎ 687-5007
Madison's Nightspot is a club that is mostly frequented by young, well-off people, mostly of Chinese origin. Cover charge is from three to five dollars. They have "Funky Fridays" and R&B and funk on Saturdays.

Piccadilly Pub
620 West Pender St.
☎ 682-3221
The best night at the Piccadilly Pub is Thursday, when groovy funk and acid-jazz make up the line-up.

Railway Club
$6 members
$8 non-members
579 Dunsmuir St.
☎ 681-1625
Folk music or blues are presented in an oblong spot that brings to mind a railway car. A miniature electric train runs in a loop above customers' heads as they enjoy the live music.

Richard's on Richards
1036 Richard St.
☎ 687-6794
Richard's on Richards is an institution in Vancouver. People of all ages flock to this chic spot to see and be seen. Theme nights. A must try.

Roxy
every day
932 Granville St.
☎*331-7999*
The Roxy is a boisterous rock club where the beer flows abundantly. Regulars include young professionals and a few cowboys. Cruising appears to be one of the favourite pastimes here. Cover charge: seven dollars.

Royal Hotel
1025 Granville St.
☎*685-5335*
A gay crowd throngs to a "modern" decor. Friday evenings are very popular, perhaps because of the live music. People wait in line as early as 5:30pm, though Sunday evenings are more worth it.

Shark Club
Mon to Sun
180 West Georgia St.
☎*687-4275*
The Shark Club is a modern bar with televisions hanging from the ceiling beaming out hockey or football games. Draft beer is the beverage of choice and baseball hats are the standard clothing accessory. Cover charge: four dollars.

Soho Café & Billiards
1144 Homer St.
☎*688-1180*
Soho Café & Billiards, one block away from the Automotive Billiards Club, is very inviting with its cozy wood and brick decor. The

pool tables are in the basement.

Starfish Room
Mon to Sat
1055 Homer St.
☎*682-4171*
The Starfish Room is a good place to hear (often very talented) live bands of various styles. Check out their ad in the *Georgia Straight* for details.

Stone Temple Cabaret
1082 Granville St.
☎*488-1333*
The Stone Temple Cabaret is a new bar in a not-too-safe part of town. 80s music on Thursdays, dance music on Saturdays and all-request Hawaiian theme on Tuesdays.

The Drink Night Club
398 Richards St.
☎*687-1307*
The Drink Night Club's DJ plans theme nights, such as Latino night, with dance lessons for beginners. Lively ambience.

Wett Bar
1320 Richards St.
☎*662-7707*
Deep jazz, funk, classic rock as well as the hits of the day. Excellent music.

Yale Hotel
1300 Granville St.
☎*681-9253*
The big names in blues regularly play at this

Entertainment

locale – the blues mecca of Vancouver. Great ambience on the weekends. The cover charge varies depending on the performers.

Yaletown Brewing Co.
1111 Mainland St.
☎681-2739
The Yaletown Brewing Co. is a popular yuppie hang-out in Yaletown and the ideal spot for an evening of brews with some friends.

Tour D: The West End

Barclay Lounge
1348 Robson St.
☎688-8850
Barclay Lounge is a cabaret-style bar connected to O'Doul's restaurant. The atmosphere is lush and the acts are talented. It's the perfect place to sip a scotch and listen to songs originally performed by Billie Holiday or Sidney Bechet.

Cia Bella
703 Denman St.
near the entrance to Stanley Park
☎668-5771
Cia Bella is a piano bar and restaurant. Its menu includes pasta, pizza and authentic Italian cuisine.

DV8
595 Davie St.
☎682-4388
A youthful 20-something crowd flocks here around 11:30pm.

Jolting Fish Billiards
201-1323 Robson St.
☎685-8015
This modern, colourful bar is smoke-free. Located on the second floor with an unobstructed view of Robson Street and two steps away from the major down-town hotels. Young, relaxed atmosphere.

Our Place Billiards
1050 Davie St.
☎682-8368
Our Place Billiards is a small room with a few tables. Regular clientele, inexpensive and friendly.

Sportscasters Bar & Grill
1400 Robson St.
☎687-0511
Sportscasters Bar & Grill offers entertainment, a game room, giant screens, grills and a dance floor. Friendly atmosphere.

Tour F: False Creek

Blue Note Jazz Bistro
2340 West Fourth Ave.
☎733-0330
Very lively from Thursday night on, this restaurant offers very good "jazz-dining". Worth visiting. Closed due to fire.

Cotton Club
200-1833 Anderson St.
at the Granville Island entrance
☎738-7465
Lively evenings filled with jazz and blues music. Sev-

eral different jazz bands every week.

The Fairview Pub
898 West Broadway St.
☎ *872-1262*
Good blues in a friendly atmosphere. Outside the downtown area. Be prepared to line up on weekends.

The Rage
750 Pacific Blvd. S.
☎ *685-5585*
The Rage is another good bar for live music. They play all styles but it's predominantly rock. Refer to the ad in the *Georgia Straight* for all the details. Open on Fridays *($5)* and Saturdays *($7)*.

Yuk Yuk's
750 Pacific Blvd., Plaza of Nations
☎ *687-5233*
Yuk Yuk's is Vancouver's famous comedy club. Varied programme; phone for details.

Tour G: Shaughnessy and South Vancouver

Lafflines Comedy Club
26 Fourth St., New Westminster
☎ *525-2262*
Located in the southeast suburbs of Vancouver, this comedy club presents local comedians. Call for details.

Tour I: The West Side

Bel Air
950 West Broadway
☎ *657-9300*
Bel Air offers good steak and beer in an intimate setting with dancing on Friday and Saturday evenings.

Culpepper's
3135 West Broadway
☎ *731-6565*
The crowd at this Irish pub sings along with the band. Convivial atmosphere, good beer and a small menu with decent fare.

Fairview
898 West Broadway
☎ *872-1262*
Fairview is the place to drink wine and beer while listening to live music; it changes several times a week. Free hors-d'oeuvres.

Rossini's Kits Beach
1525 Yew St.
☎ *737-8080*
The small outdoor terrace at Rossini's Kits Beach, which is always overflowing with people, faces the lively street that leads to the beach. The small dining room has a live jazz band every evening and serves up pasta dishes accompanied by good beer.

Entertainment

Tangerine
1685 Yew St.
☎**739-4677**
Located in the bustling
Kitsilano area, this
restaurant-bar, which has
bamboo armchairs, offers
exotic cocktails that accompany the expertly prepared
and meticulously presented
dishes. Enjoy lively music
as you dine.

Gay and Lesbian Bars

Celebrities
free admission
1022 Davie St.
☎**689-3180**
Celebrities is definitely the
best-known gay bar in
Vancouver. Straights also
come here for the music.
Drag queens make conspic-
uous appearances, espe-
cially on Wednesdays dur-
ing the female imperson-
ators night. Packed on
weekends and frequented
by an over-40 crowd.

Charlie's Lounge
455 Abbott St.
☎**685-7777**
Charlie's Lounge is a re-
laxed bar with an elegant
gay clientele, located on the
ground floor of an old
hotel. Opens at 4pm on
Mondays and Tuesdays and
at 3pm from Wednesday to
Saturday. Saturday night is
"lesbians only" and on
Sunday, they serve brunch
from 11am to 2pm. Musical
improv sessions in the

afternoon and retro dance
music at night.

Chuck's Pub
every day 11am to 1am
455 Abbott St.
☎**685-7777**
In the same hotel as Charlie's Lounge, with an
equally relaxed and elegant
atmosphere. Pub style.

Denman Station
free admission
860 Denman St.
☎**669-3448**
Denman Station is a small,
basement bar with a regular
clientele. Thursdays are
Electro Lush Lounge nights;
Fridays, High Energy Dance
Music; Saturdays, Miss
Willie Taylor's All Star Show
at 11pm; Sundays, karaoke.

Lotus Club
455 Abbott St.
☎**685-7777**
The Lotus Club is a gay bar
with a mixed clientele,
though Friday is reserved
exclusively for women. It's
located in the same hotel as
Charlie's Lounge and
Chuck's Pub, in the base-
ment.

Numbers Cabaret
$3 cover on Fri and Sat
1042 Davie St.
☎**685-4077**
Located two steps away
from Celebrities, this large
cabaret is mostly frequented
by gay men of all ages.

Odyssey
$2-$4
every day
1251 Howe St.
☎**689-5256**
The Odyssey is a gay bar where young people go to meet in a fun-loving atmosphere. GoGo Boys-Homo Homer nights on Fridays and Saturdays. Drag queens on Wednesdays and Sundays, with Feather Boa nights starting at 10pm.

Royal Hotel
1025 Granville St.
☎**685-5335**
A gay crowd throngs to a "modern" decor. Friday evenings are very popular, perhaps because of the live music. People wait in line as early as 5:30pm; Sunday evenings are a better idea.

Cultural Activities

Theatres

Art's Club Theatre
1585 Johnston
☎**687-1644**
Art's Club Theatre is a steadfast institution on the Vancouver theatre scene. Located on the waterfront on Granville Island, this theatre presents contemporary works with social themes. Audience members often get together in the theatre's bar after the plays.

Bard on the Beach
1101 Broadway W., Vanier Park
☎**737-0625 or 739-0559**
Bard on the Beach is an annual event in honour of Shakespeare. Plays are presented, all in costumes from the era, under a huge tent on a peninsula with a view of English Bay. Goes from mid-June to the end of September.

Carousel Theatre Company
1411 Cartwright St.
☎**669-3410**
The Carousel Theatre Company is also on Granville Island. It's a small well-established theatre company with a school.

Centennial Theatre Centre
2300 Lonsdale Ave., North Vancouver
☎**984-4484**
The Centennial Theatre Centre is an excellent neighbourhood theatre located in North Vancouver. The auditorium seats over 700 people and has very good acoustics. All types of shows are presented here.

Firehall Arts Centre
280 East Cordova St.
☎**689-0926**
The Firehall Arts Centre, in the east-central part of the city, has a very good reputation. Like Art's Club Theatre, it presents contemporary plays dealing with social themes. Worth a visit.

Entertainment

Green Thumb Theatre for Young People
1885 Venables St.
☎254-4055
The Green Thumb Theatre for Young People is a small theatre troupe that puts on plays for children. The theatre is in the east end of the city, close to the Vancouver East Cultural Centre.

Orpheum Theatre
Smithe St., at Seymour St.
☎665-3050
The Orpheum Theatre, dating back to the beginning of the century, doesn't look like much from the outside. On the inside, however, the rococo decor is a pleasant surprise. Most of the presentations here are musical; the Vancouver Symphonic Orchestra regularly performs here.

Queen Elizabeth Theatre
Hamilton St., at Georgia St.
☎665-3050
The Queen Elizabeth Theatre, a large hall with 2,000 seats, presents musicals and variety shows. It is also the main performance space for the Vancouver Opera.

Vancouver East Cultural Centre
1895 Venables St.
☎254-9578
"The Cultch" is an arts centre which has built a solid reputation over the years for the quality of the shows presented.

Theatre, comedy, singing and jazz; it all takes place in this cozy, dimly-lit performance space. A great experience.

Vancouver Opera
845 Cambie St.
☎682-2871
The Vancouver Opera performs at the Queen Elizabeth Theatre (see above) because Vancouver is one of the major cities in the world that doesn't have an opera house. The address here is for the administrative office which provides program information.

Vancouver Playhouse Theatre
Hamilton St. at Dunsmuir St.
☎873-3311
The Vancouver Playhouse Theatre is another multidisciplinary performance locale offering concerts, musicals and plays. The shows are always of high calibre. Worth investigating.

Vogue Theatre
918 Granville
☎331-7900
The old Vogue Theatre, renovated not long ago, follows the trend in Vancouver of presenting all types of shows: theatre, comedy, music and even film. The programming varies.

Movie Theatres

Capitol 6
820 Granville St.
☎ 669-6000
Large downtown theatre showing the latest Hollywood productions. Dolby digital sound.

CN IMAX Cinema
Second floor, Canada Place
☎ 682-IMAX
The CN IMAX Cinema consists of a seven storey-high screen and digital, 2,000-watt sound. The IMAX system is an extraordinary audiovisual experience. Call for the schedule of 3-D films being presented.

Granville 7
855 Granville St.
☎ 684-4000
The Granville 7 is located right across from the Capitol 6 and is also a large theatre showing the latest Hollywood productions. DDSS-THX sound.

Hollywood
3123 W. Broadway
☎ 738-3211
The Hollywood is a small neighbourhood theatre (Kitsilano) that shows second-run films at reasonable prices *(under $4)*.

Pacific Cinematheque
1131 Howe St.
☎ 688-8202
The Pacific Cinematheque is *the* place to go for film buffs. Information on their extensive programming is available at the Cinematheque or by phone.

Park Theatre
3440 Cambie St.
☎ 876-2747
The Park Theatre is a repertory theatre that always shows enticing films. It's located in a pleasant part of town.

Ridge Theatre
3131 Arbutus St.
☎ 738-6311
The Ridge Theatre is another repertory theatre that's located in the west end of the city. They always offer interesting films, including good-quality recent releases and foreign classics.

Vancouver Centre Cinemas
650 West Georgia St.
☎ 669-4442
The latest Hollywood productions presented in modern theatres with digital sound.

Varsity Theatre
4375 West 10th Ave.
☎ 222-2235
The Varsity Theatre, a charming little neighbourhood theatre in the west end, shows fine second-run films. Frequented mostly by people who live in the area.

Entertainment

Fifth Avenue Cinemas
2110 Burrard St.
☎734-7469
Fifth Avenue Cinemas present excellent, very recent repertory films, including many in French with English subtitles. A good spot.

Spectator Sports

Hockey

Vancouver Canucks
General Motors Place
☎899-GOAL
The Vancouver Canucks are part of the National Hockey League. They play at GM Place Stadium from October to April.

Baseball

Vancouver Canadians
Nat Bailey Stadium
☎872-5232
Vancouverites may not consider baseball their favourite sport, but the city boasts a professional team nonetheless. Games take place during the summer.

Basketball

Vancouver Grizzlies
General Motors Place
☎899-HOOP
Vancouver Grizzlies are one of the newest National Basketball Association teams.

Football

B.C. Lions
B.C. Place Stadium
☎280-4400
The B.C. Lions are part of the Canadian Football League.

Soccer

Vancouver Eighty-Sixers
Swangard Stadium
Boundary, Kingsway to Imperial
Burnaby
☎299-0086
Though many young people – including a large number of girls – play soccer here, professional teams do not draw many people. Only European immigrants attend the games at Swangard Stadium to encourage players who, for that matter, are also mainly of European origin.

Roller Hockey

Vancouver Voodoo
Pacific Coliseum
☎253-3336
Inspired by street hockey, roller hockey is a very popular sport among young boys in Vancouver. Small wonder then that a semi-professional team was formed.

Casinos

Royal Diamond Casino
750 Pacific Blvd. S.
☎ 685-2340
If you're feeling lucky, try your hand at the Royal Diamond Casino. Casinos in British Columbia are government owned with all the winnings donated to charity. A good system!

Gateway Casinos
in front of the Radisson Hotel, Burnaby
☎ 436-2211
Royal Towers Hotel, New Westminster
☎ 521-3262
You can play blackjack, roulette or mini baccarat.

Calendar of Events

January

Polar Bear Swim
every year on the morning of January 1
Hundreds of people actually choose to take a swim lasting a few minutes in the frigid waters of English Bay. If you don't feel brave enough to challenge that icy water yourself, you can always go there and watch or see it on television.

Chinese New Year
☎ 687-6021
Gung Hai Fat Choy! means "Happy New Year!" in Cantonese. The date is determined by the lunar calendar, and therefore varies every year, but celebrations are usually held around the end of January or the beginning of February. Traditional Dragon parades are organized in Chinatown and in Richmond.

Women in View
☎ 685-6684
The Women in View festival highlights the work of female performers. Theatre, dance, comedy and music are all represented. A great festival.

Pacific International Auto & Light Truck Show
BC Place Stadium
☎ 294-8330
The Pacific International Auto & Light Truck Show is the only car show in British Columbia. Over 300 vehicles of all makes. If you want to see the brand-new American models up close, this is a good opportunity.

February

The **Spring Home Show** is the biggest home show in Western Canada, which takes place under the BC Place stadium dome.

Entertainment

**South of the Border,
Candlelight & Wine**
Vancouver Hotel
☎738-6822
Every year, music and dancing liven up this joyous
evening.

March

The **BC Great Outdoors** Show
is the place to be for camping and hunting enthusiasts,
as well as for anglers.

Vancouver Storytelling Festival
for three days in March
Storytellers gather in the
West End area and practice
their art in front of a captivated audience.

April

The **Vancouver Playhouse
International Wine Festival** is
an important festival where
bottles of wine are auc-
tioned and hundreds of
wine growers gather to
discuss their art and offer
samples.

The Vancouver Sun Fun Run
takes place on the third
week of April when over
10,000 people participate in
this celebration of sports
and spring.

May

Cloverdale Rodeo. If you're in
Vancouver and have never

been to a rodeo, this is
definitely the occasion. It's
considered one of the most
important in North America.

**Vancouver International
Marathon**
☎872-2928
The Vancouver Interna-
tional Marathon starts at the
Plaza of Nations, then goes
through Stanley Park to
North Vancouver, and back
to Vancouver. Over 4,000
runners take part in this
major sporting event on the
first Sunday of May.

**Vancouver International
Children's Festival**
Vanier Park
☎687-7697
The Vancouver Interna-
tional Children's Festival
takes place the last week of
May under red and white
tents in beautiful Vanier
part. Drawing over 70,000
people each year, this big
festival is a hit with children
from all over British Columbia.

June

**Spike & Mike's Animation
Festival**
Ridge Cinema
3131 Arbutus St.
☎738-6311
Spike & Mike's Animation
Festival presents the best
animation from all over the
world every year from the
end of May to the end of
June.

International Dragon Boat Festival
False Creek
☎687-2387
Long dug-out boats in the Chinese tradition, from all over the world, compete in these friendly races on the calm waters of False Creek.

Vancouver International Jazz Festival
☎682-0706
Fans can come and satisfy their hunger for jazz at this distinguished festival. Artists perform throughout the city and the surrounding area.

Bard on the Beach
Vanier Park
☎737-0625 or 739-0559
Bard on the Beach is an annual event in honour of Shakespeare. Plays are presented under a large tent on the peninsula facing English Bay.

July

Benson & Hedges Symphony of Fire
English Bay
☎738-4304
The Benson & Hedges Symphony of Fire is an international fireworks festival. A barge on English Bay, which serves as the base of operations, is the centre of attention. Dazzling show, guaranteed thrills.

Vancouver Chamber Music Festival
☎736-6034
In the last week of July and the first week of August, six concerts are presented featuring young soloists.

Vancouver Early Music Festival
☎732-1610
The music department of the University of British Columbia (UBC) hosts a series of baroque and medieval concerts played with period instruments.

August

Vancouver Folk Music Festival
☎602-9798
The Vancouver Folk Music Festival has become a tradition in Vancouver. It takes place during the third week of August and features musicians from all over the world who play from sunrise to sunset on Jericho Beach.

Abbotsford International Airshow
Abbotsford
☎852-9011
In Abbotsford, approximately 100km east of Vancouver, both young and old will be dazzled by F-16s, F-117 Stealths, and MiGs.

Entertainment

There are also old airplanes and clothing accessories. Don't forget your aviator glasses and sunscreen.

Vancouver International Comedy Festival
☎**683-0883**

Every year on Granville Island comics provide several days of laughs.

Vancouver Fringe Festival
☎**873-3646**

The Vancouver Fringe Festival presents 10 days of theatre, including original pieces by contemporary writers.

Greater Vancouver Open
Northview Golf and Country Surry
☎**899-4641**

At the Greater Vancouver Open, the biggest names in golf compete on a splendid course.

September

Molson Indy Vancouver
BC Place Stadium, False Creek
☎**684-4639**
tickets:
☎**280-INDY**

In the heart of downtown, a course is set up where Indy racing cars (the North American equivalent of Formula 1) compete in front of 100,000 enthusiastic spectators.

Terry Fox Run
from Ceperley Park to Stanley Park
☎**464-2666**

The Terry Fox Run, a fundraising event for cancer research, takes place on foot, bicycle or roller-blades and is from one to 10km in length. The run is in memory of the young athlete, Terry Fox, who initiated it.

October

Vancouver International Film Festival
☎**685-0260**

"Hollowood North" plays host to this increasingly significant festival which offers film buffs up to 150 films from all over the world.

Vancouver International Writers and Readers Festival
☎**681-6330**

For five days during the third week of October, at least 50 writers from Canada and abroad meet with the public for conferences and readings.

November

Annual Antique Show
Vancouver Trade & Convention Centre
☎*800-667-0619*
The Annual Antique Show is an up-and-coming event featuring furniture and *objects d'art* from the 18th and 19th centuries, as well as from the beginning of the 20th.

December

**VanDusen Garden's
Festival of Lights**
☎*878-9274*
The VanDusen Garden's Festival of Lights is another festival for the whole family. Throughout the Christmas season, the VanDusen botanical garden is decorated and illuminated with lights.

Shopping

Y ou'll surely come upon all manner of interesting shops as you explore the city. To help you discover some of the best bets in Vancouver however, read on...

Malls, Department Stores and Markets

Tour A: Downtown

Pacific Centre
from Robson St. to Dunsmuir St.
☎688-7236
The Pacific Centre is the largest shopping centre in the city. Approximately 300 quality boutiques offer a complete range of everything from jewellery and clothes to top-of-the-line items. Clothing and accessories at the Hermès and Louis Vuitton boutiques in Holt Renfrew; a fitness equipment store; a Ticketmaster; The Bay and Eaton's as well as Le Château, which mainly caters to a young clientele, are all to be found here. Parking fee.

Pacific Centre Mall
corner of Howe St. and Georgia Ave.
Pacific Centre Mall is a big shopping centre located right downtown. The latest fashions from Paris to Tokyo, including of course the West Coast, are available here. There are close to 200 shops.

The Bay
at Granville and Georgia
Right downtown, this large, luxurious department store

offers over six floors of designer and brand-name clothing and accessories, a huge perfume department with Chanel, Lancôme, Saint-Laurent, Clinique and more. Its counters display precious jewellery and objects, all at very competitive prices. There are restaurants and a bar on various floors, and a catering service with coffee tables in the basement. They offer many promotions on Saturdays and Sundays.

Waterfront Centre

at the base of the Waterfront Hotel
900 Canada Pl.
Way Souvenir shops, flowers and cigars; tourist information counter; insurance company; hair salon; shoe repairs; a Starbucks coffeeshop; and a handful of small fast-food counters featuring various national cuisines.

Tour D: West End

Robson Market

Robson St. at Cardero
Robson Market has it all and then some: vegetables; fresh fish, some cleaned out; stands with fruit salads; meats, sausages and ham; pastries and other baked goods; a counter for Alsatian and German specialties; flowers and plants; vitamins and natural products; natural medicine clinic; hair salon; small

restaurants upstairs. The market is covered, but well lit.

Tour F: Burrard Inlet

Lonsdale Quay Market

123 Carries Cates Court
North Vancouver
right near the Seabus terminal
A charming market, beautiful shops, a multitude of fast-food counters – all of it made a little more lively by artists performing on the seaside terrace.

Park Royal Shopping Centre

Marine Dr., West Vancouver
5min from Lions Gate
☎925-9576
The Park Royal Shopping Centre is the most comprehensive shopping centre in West Vancouver comprising over 250 boutiques, banks, Coast Mountain and Cypress Mountain sports clothing stores as well as a Future Shop, which carries all brand-name electronics at the most competitive prices. Free parking.

Tour G: False Creek

Granville Island Market

9am to 6pm
Granville Island
Granville Island Market is Vancouver's best-known and most popular market. It is an immense commercial area surrounded by water with a fairground atmo-

sphere. Everything is available here – prepared food, organic vegetables, fresh fish and meat, wholesome breads, as well as fast-food counters and pleasant shops selling jewellery, clothing and equipment for water sports and outdoor activities. Take a day to look, sample and wander. Parking is hard to find on the street but there are two indoor parking (*fee*) lots nearby.

Tour H: South Vancouver and Shaughnessy

Oakridge Centre
Cambie St. and 41st Ave.
☎ *261-2511*
Clothing boutiques, some of which feature French or British designers such as Rodier Paris; optical wear boutique; restaurants; The Bay; Zellers. Free parking.

Aboriginal Arts and Crafts

Country Beads
2015 West Fourth Ave
☎ *730-8056*
Country Beads has thousands of pearls and books. Workshops on Aboriginal and classic necklace and bracelet making are also offered.

Inuit Gallery of Vancouver
345 Water St.
☎ *688-7323*
The Inuit Gallery of Vancouver sells some magnificent pieces of Aboriginal art from Canada's Far North and the Queen Charlotte Islands.

Khot-La-Cha
270 Whonoak St., North Vancouver
☎ *987-3339*
One block from Marine Drive and McGuire Street. Beautiful sculptures by First Nation's artists from the Salish Coast.

Leona Lattimer
1590 West Second Ave.
west of Granville Island
☎ *732-4556*
Leona Lattimer is a lovely gallery where you can admire some fine Aboriginal art or, if you like, purchase a piece. Quality jewellery and prints. Expensive.

Paint Inspirations
2003 West Fourth Ave.
☎ *735-8558*
Paint Inspirations carries all the supplies needed to paint designs on furniture or objects. You can have a lesson on the premises or buy some supplies and a video to watch at home.

The Raven and The Bear
1528 Duranleau St., Granville Island
☎ *669-3990*
Excellent-quality Aboriginal works at reasonable prices. Lithographs, sculptures and

Shopping

natural stonework.

Silver Gallery
1226 Robson St.
☎ 681-6884
The Silver Gallery is the least expensive store for fine-quality jewellery and Aboriginal crafts. Solid silver bracelets, necklaces and rings with gold enamelling can be found at competitive prices. They also sell Indonesian objects, including masks, at affordable prices.

Spirit Wrestler Gallery
8 Water St.
☎ 669-8813
Attractive sculptures and paintings by Inuit artists and artists from the northwest coast.

The Walrus & the Carpenter
1518 Duranleau St.
Granville Island Shopping Centre
☎ 687-0920
Beautiful reproductions of animals indigenous to Canada (bears, beavers, ducks).

Accessories

Delané Boutique
130 Water St.
☎ 687-1782
This shop specializes in brown and beige fine leather luggage and bags made in Canada.

I Love Hats
1509 West Broadway, at Granville St.
☎ 739-0200
All sorts of hats in all colours. Traditional, modern or fun styles. Original sunglasses too.

The Vancouver Pen Shop
512 West Hastings St.
☎ 681-1612
This speciality pen shop has all the brand names, accessories and refills imaginable.

Art Galleries

Coastal Peoples Fine Arts Gallery
1072 Mainland St.
☎ 685-9298
This brand new Yaletown shop offers an excellent selection of West Coast-style gold and silver jewellery (made on the premises), masks and totems. Personalized service.

Douglas Reynolds
2335 Granville St.
☎ 731-9292
This gallery specializing in masks has magnificent Aboriginal works of art. If the totems are too heavy to take home with you, one of the bottle mats on display will make a beautiful and affordable souvenir.

Hana Gallery
2435 Granville St.
☎ 736-8473
Hana Gallery has completely restored Japanese antiques. A memento of the way of life in Japan over the past centuries.

Marion Scott Gallery
481 Howe St.
☎ 685-1934
Marion Scott Gallery has a beautiful aboriginal art collection including superb sculptures.

Art Supplies

Maxwell's Artists' Materials
206 Cambie St. at Water St.
☎ 683-8607
As its name indicates, this shop specializes in artists' materials.

Birds

West Coast Tropical Bird
1679 West Third Ave.
☎ 733-6246
A few friendly "hellos!" welcome clients to this parakeet bird den. The birds will charm you with their colours and voices. Almost everything they need is sold here.

Bookstores

Duthie Books
2239 West Fourth Ave.
☎ 732-5344
An independent bookstore.

Douglas Coupland

Vancouver can be proud of its star-author, Douglas Coupland, who in 1991 at the age of 30 published his first novel, *Generation X*. His work coined a new catch-phrase that is now used by everyone from sociologists to ad agencies to describe this young, educated and underemployed generation.

Coupland's subsequent novels, *Shampoo Planet* (1993) *Microserfs* (1995), *Life After God* (1995), *Polaroid From the Dead* (1996), *Girlfriend in a Coma* (1997) and *Miss Wyoming* (2000) similarly contain biting social commentary.

Shopping

Little Sisters

Little Sisters Book and Art Emporium has been engaged in a long battle with Canada Customs over the importation of books that Canada Customs deems offensive. The store became a target of Canada Customs, who repeatedly opened, inspected and occasionally confiscated Little Sisters' shipments. Little Sisters took Canada Customs to B.C. Supreme Court, which ruled that Canada Customs had a right to inspect, but that the agency's conduct infringed upon gays' and lesbians' freedom of speech rights and ultimately their equality. Little Sisters continues to fight Canada Customs' methods of detention, seizure, destruction and banning of books and magazines.

Granville Book Co.
9:30am to midnight, Fri and Sat until 1am
850 Granville St.
☎*687-2213*
Right downtown on Theatre Row, Granville Book Co. carries everything from business to science fiction and fantasy books, as well as magazines.

Hagar Books
2176 West 41st Ave.
☎*263-9412*
This bookstore has been around for 25 years.

Little Sisters Book and Art Emporium
every day 10am to 11pm
1238 Davie St.
☎*669-1753 or 800-567-1662*
Little Sisters Book and Art Emporium is the only gay bookshop in Western Canada. It offers gay literature as well as essays on various subjects such as homosexuality and feminism. It is also a vast bazaar, with products that include humorous greeting cards. With the support of several Canadian literary figures, this bookshop has been fighting Canada Customs, which arbitrarily blocks the importation of certain publications. Books by recognized and respected authors such as Marcel Proust have been seized by Canada Customs, which has taken on the role of censor. Some of the same titles bound for regular bookshops have mysteri-

ously escaped seizure by Canada Customs, leading to questions about discrimination.

Chapters
788 Robson St.
☎*682-4066*
In this large bookstore, readers can peruse the latest publications, magazines and specialized books.

Oscar's Art Books & Books
1533 West Broadway, at Granville
☎*731-0533*
A large selection of fiction and books on art, cooking, nature, anatomy, travel... Wonderful books at low prices.

UBC Bookstore
6200 University Blvd.
☎*822-BOOK*
UBC Bookstore is the largest bookstore west of the Rockies with more than 100,000 titles. Allow enough time to park your car as the parking situation at UBC can be a problem.

Clothing

After Five Fashions
545 Howe St.
☎*899-0400*
Excellent selection of women's clothing. Complete outfits for business or for pleasure, not to mention formal evening dresses. Shoes and accessories also available.

Atomic Model
1036 Mainland St.
☎*688-9989*
This brand new trendy boutique imports its clothes from New York, Los Angeles, Paris and Milan.

Below the Belt
1131 Robson St.
☎*688-6878*
Below the Belt, though a bit pricey, is a favourite with fashionable teens, but also with those for whom *look* is paramount.

Dorothy Grant
757 West Hastings St.
☎*681-0201*
Dorothy Grant makes clothing styled after that of the Haida Nation. The coats and capes are especially outstanding.

Giorgio's
1055 West Georgia St.
☎*682-2228*
Giorgio's is a renowned boutique that offers a lovely selection of well-known brand names often at reasonable prices. To make you feel welcome, the staff offers you a cappuccino.

i 2 Lifestyle Retail Shop
2005 West Fourth Ave.
☎*738-2208*
i 2 Lifestyle Retail Shop is a shop that sells casual wear as well as fashion accessories, all at reasonable prices.

Just Cruisin' Shoppe
890 Howe St.
☎ 688-2030
Just Cruisin' Shoppe is one of the largest bathing-suit stores in Canada. For the entire family and all sizes.

Laura Ashley
1171 Robson St.
☎ 688-8729
Laura Ashley is an English-style women's boutique with flowered dresses and embroidered knits in pastel colours. Affordable prices.

Nicole Adrienne
2705 Granville St.
☎ 738-8187
A colourful selection of women's clothing in styles that are modern yet classic. Affordable prices.

Polo Ralph Lauren
375 Water St.
☎ 682-7656
This chic boutique has Ralph Lauren fashions for women, men and children, as well as its perfumes and jewellery.

Robin Kay
1670 Cypress St.
☎ 731-1199
Robin Kay sells 100% cotton clothing for women. From casual wear to formal dresses, all in pastel colours.

Second Suit
2036 West Fourth Ave.
☎ 732-0338
Second Suit carries the best in formal menswear from Armani to Boss and Dior.

Tilley Endurables Western
2041 Granville St., corner Eight Ave.
☎ 732-4287
From safari jackets and patch pocket pants to vests and hats for rainy or sunny weather, this store's refined attire, made from weather-resistant material, is suitable for strolls or longer excursions.

True Value Vintage
710 Robson St.
☎ 685-5403
True Value Vintage is an exceptional shop that both buys and sells vintage clothing from the glory days of rockabilly and disco.

Vizio
128-1208 Homer St.
☎ 899-1208
Vizio sells beautiful fashion accessories and clothing of all kinds imported from Europe and Asia.

Tailors

Royal Custom Tailors
2427 Granville St.
☎ 736-1727
Royal Custom Tailors is a small tailor shop of the kind that is rarely seen these days. You can order a custom-made suit, have your zipper changed or get your pants hemmed for only a few dollars.

Electronics

A&B Sound
556 Seymour St.
☎687-5837
A&B Sound has great prices in electronics, video cassettes and compact discs. Watch out for the crowds on weekends.

Flowers

Eden Florist
843 Davie St.
☎685-8058
Eden Florist specializes in flowers for all occasions. Personalized service and free delivery.

Food

Capers
1675 Robson St.
☎687-5288
Capers is a natural food store that carries fresh vegetables, meats, prepared dishes, good breads and vitamins. Somewhat expensive but practical for travellers. You can eat here.

Chocolat Daniel
1105 Robson St.
☎688-9624
One of the rare fine-chocolate shops in Vancouver, and probably the best. The dark chocolate and truffles, prepared in strict Belgian tradition, are exceptional.

Small figurines, boxes and vases enhance their presentation and make lovely gifts. The prices are reasonable. There are seven more Chocolat Daniels throughout the city; call the number listed above for their locations.

Chocolate Arts
2037 West Fourth Ave.
☎739-0475
Chocolate Arts is renowned for its high quality chocolate as well as its elegant creations whose shapes are inspired by West Coast Ab-original art.

Kobayashi Shoten
1518 Robson St.
☎683-1019
This Japanese store sells groceries, take-out meals and gifts as well as table settings and linens.

Leysley Stowe
1780 West Third Ave., corner Burrard St.
☎731-3663
Leysley Stowe is a gourmet grocer and caterer that sells cheeses and other fine products from France. The breads and cakes are always fresh.

Meinhardt
3002 Granville St.
☎732-4405
Another health-food store. Same formula as Capers but smaller, with more of a family atmosphere. They sell Godiva chocolates and

Shopping

lovely fresh flowers. A bit expensive.

Rocky Mountain Chocolate Factory
1017 Robson St.
☎688-4100
Rocky Mountain Chocolate Factory is a divine little chocolate shop. You can savour bulk chocolate with nuts and fruits, or perhaps the bitter dark chocolate, for the real connoisseur.

Ten Ren Tea and Ginseng Company
550 Main St.
☎684-1566
The Ten Ren Tea and Ginseng Company is without a doubt the best tea shop in Canada. Big jars hold an exceptional variety of teas from around the world.

Jade World
by appointment only
Suite 403 - 1311 Howe St.
☎733-7212
Right near Granville Island. Jade sculptures and jewellery

Rasta Wares
1505 Commercial Dr.
☎255-3600
This shop offers incense and jewellery from India, Indonesia and Africa at low prices.

Wendy's Collection
2620 West Broadway
☎730-8381
The window catches your eye from a distance. The shop sells superb statuettes and sculptures from China. Jewellery and gemstones at affordable prices.

Gifts

Alders Duty-Free
1026 Alberni St.
Internationally renowned, brand-name cosmetics, jewellery, leather goods, liquor and tobacco – all tax-free for tourists from outside Canada.

Crystal Gallery
Lonsdale Quay Market
North Vancouver
☎986-8224
Reasonably priced, attractive, brightly coloured crystal objects.

Glasses and Contact Lenses

Eyes on Burrard
775 Burrard St.
☎688-9521
This shop, which specializes in designer frames, also has a few well-known brand names of tinted lenses.

Lenscrafters
Pacific Centre
☎685-1024
One-hour service, efficient and reliable; wide selection of fashionable frames.

Regency Contact Lens
607-650 West 41st Ave., Oakridge Center
entrance on Cambie St.
☎*263-0900*
Contact lens specialists, offering quality service and competitive prices.

Yaletown Optical
1051 Mainland St.
☎*684-1243*
Yaletown Optical offers lovely frames as well as well-known brand names of trendy glasses.

Hairdressers

Suki's Hair Salon
3157 S. Granville St., at 16th Ave.
☎*738-7713*
Vancouver's most fashionable hair salon, frequented by the jetset. They offer a wide range of services at affordable prices.

Home Decor and Accessories

Hana Gallery
2435 Granville St.
☎*736-8473*
One of the rare stores selling Japanese antiques. Beautiful furniture and accessories imported from Japan.

Kaya Kaya
2039 West Fourth Ave.
☎*732-1816*
Kaya Kaya has Japanese porcelain and other Japanese accessories for the home, some of which are genuine works of art.

Kim-John
2903 Granville St., at 13th Ave.
☎*732-7311*
Articles for your house and dining-room table in fine Chinese or British porcelain (Wedgewood, Royal Doulton), Bohemian crystal or solid silver at 50% off regular prices. A multitude of attractive, affordably priced objects.

The Kitchen Corner
2686 Granville St.
☎*739-4422*
You'll find absolutely everything in this little store for next to nothing: anything you might need for your kitchen, for camping, a day at the beach as well as spices, candles, souvenirs...

Light Effects
2412 Granville St.
☎*730-9100*
Light Effects has hundreds of colourful lamps of all shapes and sizes, all of which are imitations of popular styles. Very reasonable prices.

Mihrab
2229 Granville St.
☎*879-6105*
Mihrab sells carved doors, antique furniture, pillars, bronzes and carpets. You will find all the charm of southern Asia in this store.

Shopping

Ming Wo Cookware
2066 and 2170 West Fourth Ave.
☎ **737-2624**
You will find every kitchen utensil imaginable at these two stores. With their cheery, modern shapes and colours, the spoons, forks and even the garbage cans make attractive accessories. Very reasonable prices.

Scandinavia Arts
648 Hornby St.
☎ **688-9898**
Scandinavia Arts specializes in high-quality Scandinavian crystal. The modern designs are elegant. Besides the well-known brand names, it also offers less expensive crystal creations.

The Spirit of Christmas
right at the corner of
Robson St. and Bute St.
take the stairs
☎ **683-2507**
The Spirit of Christmas is the largest store in Canada solely devoted to Christmas. The selection and beauty of the decorations is amazing.

Leather

Marte's Fine Leather
134-1055 West Georgia St., Royal Centre
☎ **684-6424**
Marte's Fine Leather is a leather shop that has luggage and overnight cases as well as briefcases and handbags.

Ocean Drive Leather
1060 Mainland
☎ **647-2244**
Located in the new Yaletown area, Ocean has fashionable leather clothing for men and women.

Lingerie

La Jolie Madame
Pacific Centre
Fourth floor in the Atrium
☎ **669-1831**
Fine lingerie and negligées for women and young ladies. Well-known brands imported from Paris.

Music

Highlife Records & Music
1317 Commercial Dr.
☎ **251-6964**
This is the spot to find new wave and other types of music at good prices.

HMV
1160 Robson St.
HMV is the mega-store for music, with great prices on new releases. The store is open late on weekends.

Long & McQuade Limited Musical Instruments
2301 Granville St.
☎ **734-4886**
Long & McQuade Limited Musical Instruments has all sorts of musical instruments, both new and used, are for sale or for rent for a day, month or year.

Not Just Another Music Shop
2415 Granville St.
☎733-6526
It has an excellent selection of new and used guitars. Rentals, repairs and guitar lessons.

Virgin Megastore
788 Burrard St.
☎669-2289

Newspapers and Magazines

Magpie Magazine Gallery
Mon to Fri 10am to 10pm
Sat and Sun 10am to 7pm
1319 Commercial Dr.
☎253-6666

Mayfair News
1535 West Broadway
☎738-8951
Newspapers and magazines from all over the world in every language are found here, sometimes a bit later than the original issue date.

Pharmacies

Gaia Garden Herbal Apothecary
2672 West Broadway
☎734-4372
The only place in town that has everything in the way of herbal medicines. Visa cards accepted.

Shoppers Drug Mart
many locations throughout the city
the following two are open 24hrs/day
1125 Davie St.
☎669-2424
2302 West Fourth Ave.
☎738-3138
Shoppers Drug Mart has a bit of everything: pharmacist, cosmetics, items for the home, pop, juice, a few groceries.

Tung Fong Hung
536 Main St.
☎688-0883
Tung Fong Hung is a traditional Chinese herbalist. Ask for Liping, who will take the time to explain the complex healing powers of these plants. The shop specializes in ginseng.

Photocopies and Office Supplies

Kinko's
1900 West Broadway
☎734-2679
If you need to use a computer, make some photocopies or simply buy some office supplies, this store is open 24hrs.

Shoes

David Gordon
822 Granville St.
☎685-3784
David Gordon is a typical western shoe store with

Shopping

boots, shoes and sandals. It's been in business since 1976 and has a good reputation.

Stéphane de Raucourt Shoes
1067 Robson St.
☎681-8814
If you are looking for quality shoes that stand out from the ordinary, here is a spot to keep in mind. They are expensive, but a little window-shopping never hurt anyone.

Tallcrest Shoes
644 Hornby St.
☎669-3738
From sports shoes to dress shoes. This store specializes in large sizes.

Western Town Boots
2940 Main St.
☎879-1914
All kinds of cowboy and cowgirl boots in all sizes.

Souvenirs

Great Canadian Garment & Gift Company
213 Carrall St.
☎684-2270
Located in the Gastown area, this shop sells clothing embroidered with the colour of the Canadian flag, as well as other items made in Canada.

Robson Souvenirs Centre
1222 Robson St.
☎683-9686
Robson Souvenirs Centre offers a wide selection of Canadian, North American and Aboriginal souvenirs. They also sell smoked and canned salmon, as well as maps and travel guides of the area.

Sports and the Outdoors

Altus Mountain Gear
137 West Broadway
☎876-5255
Altus Mountain Gear carries everything for mountaineering: waterproof gear, clothing, tents, backpacks and more at cost price or for rent.

Coast Mountain Sports
2201 West Fourth Ave.
☎731-6181
A stop at Coast Mountain Sports is a must for mountaineers who appreciate quality equipment. Only the best is sold here; the shop is therefore quite expensive and reserved mostly for pros. The staff is very friendly and experienced.

Comor Go Play Outside
1918 Fir St.
☎731-2163
Everything for outdoor sports, especially cycling and skateboarding. Equipment, clothing, helmets, shoes and more.

Cyclepath
1421 West Broadway
one block east of Granville St.
☎737-2344
This bike shop does repairs
and sells all sorts of bicycles
and accessories.

Ecomarine Granville Island
1668 Duranleau St.
☎689-7575
Ecomarine Granville Island
has everything for fans of
sea-kayaking. You can even
try out the kayaks before
you buy.

Mountain Equipment Co-op
130 West Broadway
☎872-7858
Mountain Equipment Co-op
is a gigantic store that offers
everything you need for
your outdoor activities. You
must be a member to make
purchases; but membership
only costs $5.

Ruddick's Fly Fishing
1654 Duranleau St., Granville Island
☎681-3747
Ruddick's Fly Fishing is a
wonderful store for fly-fishing fans that even inspires
newcomers to the sport.
There are thousands of
different flies for all sorts of
fish. The owner will be glad
to assist you. They also sell
super-light canes, state-of-
the-art fishing reels, souvenir clothing as well as
fishing-related sculptures
and gadgets.

Nevada Bob's
230 SW Marine Dr.
☎324-1144
Nevada Bob's is one of the
largest golf stores in
Canada. There are a dozen
locations in Vancouver. If
you can't find what you
want at this location, the
manager will find it for you
at another one.

Taiga Works
390 West Eighth Ave.
☎875-6640
Taiga Works is a small shop
with mountain sports equipment and prices that beat
the competition. Gore-Tex
is at half-price. A good address to remember.

3 Vets
2200 Yukon St.
☎872-5475
3 Vets is a local institution.
For 40 years this store has
been supplying reasonably
priced camping equipment
to everyone from profes-
sional lumberjacks to tree
planters and weekend
campers.

Stationery

Kinko's Copies
24hrs/day
1900 West Broadway
☎734-2679
Computers and photocopy
machines, as well as paper
and office supplies. Everything you could possibly
need (at low prices) to create CV's, files and docu-

Shopping

ments. Very knowledgeable staff.

Tea and Natural Products

Deserving Thyme
1340 Davie St.
☎683-7796
In a calm ambience with a grey and green decor, this store offers essential oils and fine herbal teas. A good selection of candles scented with energizing and relaxing fragrances.

Finlandia
1964 West Broadway
☎733-5323
This store has an excellent selection of vitamins, herbs and essential oils, as well as homeopathic products to gently cure what ails you. It's also a traditional pharmacy. Personalized, friendly service.

Murchie's Teas & Coffees
City Square, 555 West 12th Ave.
☎872-4750
970 Robson St.
☎681-4150
These two downtown locations carry a vast, unbeatable selection of teas and coffees that has given Murchie's its solid West Coast reputation.

Telephones and Telecommunications

Cell City Communications
105-950 West Broadway
☎737-8018
You can rent a cellular phone, a pager or obtain other services that will put you in reach at any time of day.

Communication Solutions
1199 West PenderSt.
☎662-3931
If you need a cellular phone for the duration of your stay or just for a day, this store will cater to your needs.

Index

Travel Notes

Travel Notes

Travel Notes

_____

_____

_____

_____

_____

_____

_____

_____

_____

_____

_____

_____

_____

_____

_____

_____

_____

_____

_____

_____

_____

Travel Notes

Order Form

Ulysses Travel Guides

☐ Atlantic Canada	$24.95 CAN $17.95 US
☐ Bahamas	$24.95 CAN $17.95 US
☐ Beaches of Maine	$12.95 CAN $9.95 US
☐ Bed & Breakfasts in Québec	$14.95 CAN $10.95 US
☐ Belize	$16.95 CAN $12.95 US
☐ Calgary	$17.95 CAN $12.95 US
☐ Canada	$29.95 CAN $21.95 US
☐ Chicago	$19.95 CAN $14.95 US
☐ Chile	$27.95 CAN $17.95 US
☐ Colombia	$29.95 CAN $21.95 US
☐ Costa Rica	$27.95 CAN $19.95 US
☐ Cuba	$24.95 CAN $17.95 US
☐ Dominican Republic	$24.95 CAN $17.95 US
☐ Ecuador and Galapagos Islands	$24.95 CAN $17.95 US
☐ El Salvador	$22.95 CAN $14.95 US
☐ Guadeloupe	$24.95 CAN $17.95 US
☐ Guatemala	$24.95 CAN $17.95 US
☐ Honduras	$24.95 CAN $17.95 US
☐ Las Vegas	$17.95 $12.95
☐ Lisbon	$18.95 CAN $13.95 US
☐ Louisiana	$29.95 CAN $21.95 US
☐ Martinique	$24.95 CAN $17.95 US
☐ Montréal	$19.95 CAN $14.95 US
☐ Miami	$9.95 CAN $12.95 US
☐ New Orleans	$17.95 CAN $12.95 US
☐ New York City	$19.95 CAN $14.95 US
☐ Nicaragua	$24.95 CAN $16.95 US

☐ Ontario	$27.95 CAN
	$19.95US
☐ Ottawa	$17.95 CAN
	$12.95 US
☐ Panamá	$24.95 CAN
	$17.95 US
☐ Peru	$27.95 CAN
	$19.95 US
☐ Portugal	$24.95 CAN
	$16.95 US
☐ Provence - Côte d'Azur	$29.95 CAN
	$21.95US
☐ Puerto Rico	$24.95 CAN
	$17.95 US
☐ Québec	$29.95 CAN
	$21.95 US
☐ Québec and Ontario with Via	$9.95 CAN
	$7.95 US
☐ Seattle	$17.95 CAN
	$12.95 US
☐ Toronto	$18.95 CAN
	$13.95 US
☐ Vancouver	$17.95 CAN
	$12.95 US
☐ Washington D.C.	$18.95 CAN
	$13.95 US
☐ Western Canada	$29.95 CAN
	$21.95 US

Ulysses Due South

☐ Acapulco	$14.95 CAN
	$9.95 US
☐ Belize	$16.95 CAN
	$12.95 US
☐ Cancún & Riviera Maya	$19.95 CAN
	$14.95 US
☐ Cartagena (Colombia)	$12.95 CAN
	$9.95 US
☐ Huatulco - Puerto Escondido	$17.95 CAN
	$12.95 US
☐ Los Cabos and La Paz	$14.95 CAN
	$10.95 US
☐ Puerto Vallarta	$14.95 CAN
	$9.95 US
☐ St. Martin and St. Barts	$16.95 CAN
	$12.95 US

Ulysses Travel Journals

☐ Ulysses Travel Journal (Blue, Red, Green, Yellow, Sextant)	$9.95 CAN
	$7.95 US
☐ Ulysses Travel Journal 80 Days	$14.95 CAN
	$9.95 US

Ulysses Green Escapes

☐ Cycling in France . . . . $22.95 CAN
$16.95 US
☐ Cycling in Ontario . . . . $22.95 CAN
$16.95 US
☐ Hiking in the . . . . $19.95 CAN
Northeastern U.S. $13.95 US
☐ Hiking in Québec . . . . $19.95 CAN
$13.95 US

Title	Qty	Price	Total
Name:		Subtotal	
		Shipping	$4 CAN
Address:		Subtotal	
		GST in Canada 7%	
		Total	
Tel: Fax:			
E-mail:			
Payment: ☐ Cheque ☐ Visa ☐ MasterCard			
Card number_____ Expiry date_____			
Signature_____			

ULYSSES TRAVEL GUIDES
4176 St-Denis,
Montréal, Québec, H2W 2M5
(514) 843-9447 fax (514) 843-9448
Toll free: 1-877-542-7247
Info@ulysses.ca
www.ulyssesguides.com